Exploring Theatre and Education

Edited by KEN ROBINSON

With contributions by
Dorothy Heathcote
William Gaskill
Gavin Bolton
Nicholas Wright
Gerald Chapman
John Dale

HEINEMANN
LONDON

Heinemann Educational Books Ltd
22 Bedford Square, London WC1B 3HH
LONDON EDINBURGH MELBOURNE AUCKLAND
HONG KONG SINGAPORE KUALA LUMPUR NEW DELHI
IBADAN NAIROBI JOHANNESBURG
EXETER(NH) KINGSTON PORT OF SPAIN

First published 1980

British Library C.I.P. Data
Riverside Drama Conference, *London, 1978*
    Exploring theatre and education.
    1. Drama in education – Great Britain – Congresses
    2. Theater – Great Britain – Congresses
    I. Title   II. Robinson, Ken
    792',07'1041   PN3171
    ISBN 0-435-18780-5
    ISBN 0-435-18781-3 Pbk

Printed and bound in Great Britain by
Spottiswoode Ballantyne Ltd, Colchester and London

Contents

Notes on the Contributors

DOROTHY HEATHCOTE teaches at the University of Newcastle School of Education taking in-service and graduate courses in drama in education. Her work with children is internationally known and has been the subject of two documentary films in the BBC *Omnibus* series – *Three Looms Waiting* and *Seeds of a New Life*. A full length book on her work by Betty Jane Wagner – *Dorothy Heathcote: Drama as an Educational Medium* has been published in Britain by Hutchinson (1979).

WILLIAM GASKILL was Associate Director of the National Theatre from 1963–1965 and Artistic Director of the Royal Court from 1965–1975 during which time he directed many of Brecht's plays and most of Edward Bond's early work. He has directed in Germany, Australia and the United States. His recent productions include *Fan Shen* with the Joint Stock Company in 1975; *The Ragged Trousered Philanthropists* in 1978; *A Fair Quarrel* at the Olivier in 1979; and *The Gorky Brigade* at the Royal Court in 1979.

GAVIN BOLTON teaches at the University of Durham School of Education and, like Dorothy Heathcote, has an international reputation in drama in education having lectured throughout Britain, Canada, Australia and in the United States. He is author of *Towards a Theory of Drama in Education* (Longmans, 1980) and of numerous articles and contributions to the literature of the arts in education.

NICHOLAS WRIGHT was born in 1940 in Cape Town and has worked in London for twenty years as actor, director and playwright. He was on the staff of the Royal Court from 1968–1976 working variously as Casting Director, Assistant Director and Joint Artistic Director. For five years he ran the Theatre

Upstairs during which time it became the centre of the new writing of the first half of the 1970s. His own plays are *Changing Lines* (Royal Court, 1969), *Treetops* (Riverside Studios, 1978) and *The Gorky Brigade* (Royal Court, 1979).

GERALD CHAPMAN worked as a trainee director at the Theatre Royal, York and the Haymarket Theatre, Leicester, subsequently running a professional community theatre company in South East London. He has worked freelance at Lincoln Theatre Royal, the Theatre at New End in London, the Institute of Contemporary Arts and at the Almost Free Theatre where he directed a play in Gay Sweatshop's first season. He joined the Royal Court in June 1976 as director of the Young People's Theatre Scheme.

JOHN DALE trained as a teacher and worked for several years as an actor in Theatre in Education. He directed a community arts centre for young people bringing together professional actors, musicians and art/craft specialists. He has written several plays for young audiences and devised the music for four major children's shows. While at the Royal Court he directed four youth theatre productions based on new play commissions. He is now a writer and director for children's television at the BBC.

KEN ROBINSON was a member of the national research and development project on the teaching of drama funded by the Schools Council. He was co-author of *Learning Through Drama* (Heinemann Educational Books, 1977). He has lectured extensively in Great Britain and abroad and contributed to many journals and books on drama, theatre and the arts in education.

Introduction

Shortly after they opened in 1978, the Riverside Studios in London were taken over for a working conference called simply, *Theatre – Education: An Exploration.* The conference was organized by Gerald Chapman and John Dale, the directors of the Young People's Theatre Scheme at the Royal Court and was funded by the Greater London Arts Association.

It was prompted by the lack of contact between the professional theatre and those involved in drama teaching and by a recognition that theatre work which did claim an educational function – Children's Theatre, Youth Theatre and Theatre in Education – was still thought by many of those in 'mainstream theatre' to be unconnected with, or unimportant to, what they themselves were doing. On top of this many drama teachers, through their general concern to encourage self-expression by children, had come at various times in the past to wonder if teaching children about plays and the theatre was really part of their work at all. The effect of all this seemed to be a widening abyss between educational drama and the various aspects of the professional theatre.

The conference set out to initiate a debate on these issues by bringing together a large audience of directors, teachers, actors, educational advisers and actor/teachers, to compare two methods of work: theatre directing and drama teaching. They were invited first, to see if there were any shared elements and second, to draw from their observations any conclusions about the nature of theatre and of educational drama that might suggest an important relationship between the arts and education in general.

It was hoped to establish both the differences and the common ground between theatre and drama teaching and to propose ways in which the arts and education might cooperate more fully with each other.

Three distinguished practitioners were invited to demonstrate aspects of their work to the conference. Gavin Bolton and

Dorothy Heathcote worked with groups of children for three one-and-a-half-hour sessions: Dorothy Heathcote with a group of fourth years from a local comprehensive school and Gavin Bolton with a first year group from the same school.[1] William Gaskill worked with a group of actors and actresses also for three sessions. The audience was divided into three and during the two days of the conference had an opportunity to see each of the demonstration working groups for one session. Thus group A, for example, saw William Gaskill's opening session with the actors on Saturday morning, Dorothy Heathcote's second session with the children on Saturday afternoon and Gavin Bolton's third session with the children on Sunday morning. Dorothy Heathcote also worked with the actors' group for one session on the Sunday afternoon. On the second day all members of the conference had the chance to get together in mixed groups to discuss and compare the work they had seen. The conference ended with a full plenary discussion. The weekend also included performances of *Class Enemy* by Nigel Williams at the Royal Court Theatre.

Broadly speaking the terms of this book are the same as for the conference itself. But this is not just a straightforward record of what happened there. Not surprisingly it did not end with a neat set of conclusions and a round of hearty applause. On some issues there was warm agreement, on others heated division. Over all there was a feeling that the debate which the conference had ignited should be kept alive and be fuelled by further elaboration from those whose work had been seen, of the practical points they were trying to make and their reasons for working as they do. The many issues which had been raised about theatre and educational drama in general also needed to be investigated further.

This is what this book sets out to do. It is a development of the Riverside Conference and not just its archive. It is really in two parts reflecting two broad aims. The first three chapters describe and analyse in some detail the practical work which was done at the conference itself and aim to explore the general issues of the book through comparing the working methods of Dorothy Heathcote, Bill Gaskill and Gavin Bolton. Each was asked at the beginning of the conference to make an introductory statement about their work in general and what they hoped to cover during the course of the weekend. These statements are incorporated into the three chapters, each of which is structured slightly differently.

Chapter 1 begins with a general statement from Dorothy Heathcote on the principles underlying her work in drama. She sees no dichotomy between theatre and drama activities in education, and conceives of the role of the drama teacher as being close to that of the playwright and director as described by Brecht. Each of her three sessions with the children is outlined and the first session is presented in detail together with an analysis of her actions as the session leader. This takes the form of a narrative of the external events of the session, including transcripts of her interaction with the group, interleaved with questions which I put to her later, asking for clarification of her thinking and methods at different points in the work. Her session with the actors proved to be the most controversial of the conference and polarized opinion on her work. This session is presented in the same way and the chapter closes with her own postscript on the conference dealing particularly with the role of actors working in schools and the issues facing future cooperation between education and theatre.

William Gaskill's work is described and analysed in Chapter 2 using the same format: it begins with an introductory statement on the changing role of the director and then moves into a presentation of his three sessions, the first being considered in greater detail through questions put to him on general methods and specific principles. He argues that in contrast to the apparent emphasis on 'universality' and 'looking for significance' in the drama work he saw at the conference, working in theatre involves dealing always with specifics and resisting temptations to generalize.

Gavin Bolton reviews his own work at the conference and deals particularly with the criticism raised there that he actually seemed to be suppressing the children's creative energies by excessive talk, and so subverting opportunities for self-expression. He describes the use of theatre form in the teaching of drama, the nature of the children's emotional involvement in the lesson and the principal functions of the drama teacher. He rejects attempts to oversimplify the relationship between drama and theatre arguing that, unless we recognize certain crucial differences between them, we can never usefully exploit the common ground.

Chapters 3–6 are somewhat different: they aim to consider some of the more general issues which were raised at the conference to do with the roles, functions ánd methods of work in educational drama and the theatre and take the weekend as a reference point rather than as the principal focus.

Nicholas Wright is a playwright and director. He was invited to look at the work of the conference, to listen to the discussions and to respond to them as a professional theatre worker. He takes issue with whole idea of universals in drama teaching as put forward by Dorothy Heathcote and criticizes the 'mistaken emphasis' on subjectivity in much of the work. He describes the playwright's attempts to limit the meaning of a play through the conscious use of form and the way in which this makes statements in the theatre objective, relative and refutable so far as the audience is concerned. In contrast to this, the premium placed on subjectivity and self-expression in the drama lessons, he argues, simply opens the door for ever more subtle forms of indoctrination by the teacher.

In Chapter 5 Gerald Chapman looks at the functions of theatre work specifically for and with young people. He attacks what he sees as the complacent and patronizing attitude of much of the professional theatre to work with young people arguing that the 'political cutting edge' of contemporary theatre is primarily centred on such work. He traces the history of the Young People's Theatre Scheme at the Royal Court as an example of the general difficulties facing this work and describes the principles which now underpin the scheme and the specific activities by which they are put into practice.

In Chapter 6 I argue that the dichotomy between educational drama and theatre has been opened up because of a mistaken emphasis, by educationalists, on self-expression and individuality and that this has blurred some of the most important functions of the arts in schools. It is part of drama teachers' responsibility to help children to understand and participate in theatre activities. The emphasis on creativity and self-expression as a way of developing individuality may be having just the opposite effect.

In bringing this book together I have not tried to settle the debate at Riverside or to offer formal conclusions which it lacked. Each of the contributors writes on their own behalf and there is no party line. The same issues tend to recur but they are handled very differently. The intention rather has been to probe more deeply into the arguments and attitudes which surround this debate and to relate it to more general questions.

It is important to understand that there is a general question here and that we are not just concerned with some sort of domestic squabble between theatres and schools. There is a sense of distance and remoteness between arts education and professional artists right across the board: in dance and dance education, music and music education, art and art education and so on. The general question can take a number of forms.

If the point of arts education is to encourage self-expression and creativity, as many have claimed it is, does this mean that teaching children to understand and appreciate realized art forms – paintings, plays, literature – is less important that it was formerly thought to be in schools? Are self-expression and creativity really the point of arts education? When we ask children to be creative in schools, as in drama say, are they involved in exactly the same process which professional artists go through in their own work? If not, what are the differences, and are they important? Does all of this creative activity, in schools or in theatres and galleries have a purpose or is it just a 'good thing'? What is the role of the teacher in drama? Is it the same as the director in the theatre? Or the playwright? Or what? Should children be encouraged to perform in schools? Should actors? Does the work of professional theatre have a function for children – or anyone else – and how important is it for the future vitality of the arts that rising generations be taught to appreciate 'the cultural heritage'?

Many of these issues hinge on the apparently rival claims for appreciation – that is, what others do – and participation – that is, doing it yourself. The current movement in community arts has raised just this issue outside the formal structures of education. Should the Arts Council, many now ask, be encouraging a popular involvement in arts activities by funding more community groups, more arts centres, more T.I.E. teams, more Youth Theatres and so on? Or should it continue to sponsor 'centres of excellence' and prestigious professional artists as its main priority? Poor central funding means that it can hardly afford to do both and for many people this has now become a straight choice between a policy of 'cultural democracy' and 'cultural elitism' on the one hand and sacrificing or preserving the 'cultural heritage' on the other.

In his opening remarks at the Riverside Conference, Roy Shaw the current Secretary General of the Arts Council said:

> It is sometimes forgotten that the Arts Council of Great Britain has more than one aim. Its most commonly known aim is 'to increase the accessibility of the arts to the public'. But we tend to forget – and perhaps the Arts Council itself tends to forget – its other aims: 'To develop and improve knowledge, understanding and practice of the arts.' That is an educational task. To divorce educational policy from cultural policy is to cripple both.[2]

This seems wise. But does it mean that schools and colleges should help keep up a supply of appreciative audiences for professional artists to play to and thus guarantee their survival? Or does it mean that the artists themselves should muck in with the business of education and help out in the schools? Or both? Are these two worlds connected, interdependent or quite separate?

Successive reports on the arts, including those of the T.U.C. and Labour and Conservative parties, have argued that the arts must be seen as an integral part of social life. The T.U.C. report argues that for this to happen the arts must be put on the political agenda along with housing and education.[3] Lord Redcliffe-Maud in his report to the Gulbenkian Foundation on *Support for the Arts*[4] argued that without a coherent policy of arts work in schools, the rising generation would perhaps have less of an interest in the survival of the arts than many of the present generation seem to have. The arts and education, he said, are 'natural allies'.

But in what sense are they allies and what form should this alliance take? In the chapters which follow, these issues are approached through a close examination of the work itself. Bill Gaskill says in his opening remarks that few people understood the ideas of Stanislavsky until reading actual details of what he did in practice. This book follows that example. So: are the professional arts and arts education rooted in the same ways of working and on the same principles? What of this relationship between drama and theatre?

KEN ROBINSON

1. From the Particular to the Universal

Dorothy Heathcote

Robert Frost, when asked by a budding poet what he thought of the young man's work – the young man already considering himself to be a poet – said, 'Poet is a gift word. You cannot give it to yourself.' I think the same is true of 'teacher'. Some days I am given it and some days I do not earn the right to be in the lists at all.

For a long time I have known that I am an 'amateur' in educational circles. By this I mean that I always feel that, beside other people's thinking and talk, I stick out like a sore thumb. I read another book recently, however, and was immediately heartened by the realization that my 'amateurishness', comes from my never having learned the language of depersonalization. Perhaps that accounts for why I am so bad at explaining what I am about to do and afterwards why I did what I did. I always understand it very clearly but find it difficult to depersonalize it in explanations. So do we slowly grow into understanding and change our perspectives ever so slightly, inch by inch.

The following quotations illuminate for me three important aspects of the teacher's work. The teacher's reason for the work done is summed up for me by Josephine Miles: 'I think that an art gives shape and stability to the valued materials of life, in order that they may be stressed, attended to and preserved.'[1] That is at the root of the way I work.

The rights of all my students – children, adults and of myself – are clarified for me in De Quincey's words: 'It is the grandeur of all truth which can occupy a very high place in human interest, that it is never absolutely novel to the meanest of minds; it exists by way of germ or latent principle in the lowest as in the highest, needing to be developed but never planted.'[2] I believe that every child I meet understands deep, basic matters worthy of exploration but they may as yet have no language for them. One of the languages they may develop is through dramatic work. As yet we do not give this grace freely to all our students. Often we deny to others that which we value for ourselves.

The relationship of artistic endeavour to the ordinary, and the awesome, in our lives is summed up for me by Stanley Kunitz: 'No poetry is *required* of any of us. Our first labour is to master our worlds.'[3] This sounds so dull until you place 'ordinary' beside 'awsome'. Then you realize the roots of poetry and all high endeavours which grow out of the need to understand – to explain things to ourselves. What a privilege to be there when a bit of understanding happens to someone!

I am concerned, in my teaching, with the difference in reality between the real world where we seem to 'really exist' and the 'as if' world where we can exist at will. I do live but I may also say, 'If it were like this, this is how I would live.' *It is the nature of my teaching to create reflective elements within the existence of reality.* Brecht calls this 'visiting another room'.

The main differences between actions in these two rooms are to do with:

1. The freedom to experiment without the burden of future repercussions.
2. The absence of the 'chance element' of real life.

If we needed a *reasonable* reason for including the arts in schools, surely it is here in these two rooms. But they are not depersonalized and it is because the schooling system is, for the most part, that they are not valued as yet. I wonder if they ever can be? What changes in our aspirations for our future and for our culture will have to come about before they are?

The thesis of Erving Goffman's book *Frame Analysis*[4] is that the real world of sociology has embraced terms which the theatre has used for many generations because theatre, like sociology, seeks to examine the nature of social life. He looks at how we function socially in the roles of participant and spectator and talks about different 'framings' of experience. The key word in his analysis is 'purity' which he uses descriptively rather than judgmentally. The road from existing *in* your life to demonstrating *how* life is lived can be thought of as a continuum, thus:

'I live   .   .   .   .   I show how life is lived.'

Between these two poles there are many different types of social situations in which we have to find our way. In doing this we read signals in the events of which we are part and place them within a particular frame of reference. This guides us in our actions and responses. In some situations our behaviour is, to a high degree, fixed and pre-ordained by traditions, circumstance and the very nature of the event, particularly whether it is private or public.

Goffman divides the various types of situation into 'bands' (see Figure 1). The most formalized situations he calls the most 'pure'. By this he means that in them our behaviour is strictly pre-ordained and chance, or random behaviour, is reduced to a minimum. Broadly speaking, the more public the event, the more planning it will require so that 'fitting' things are done.

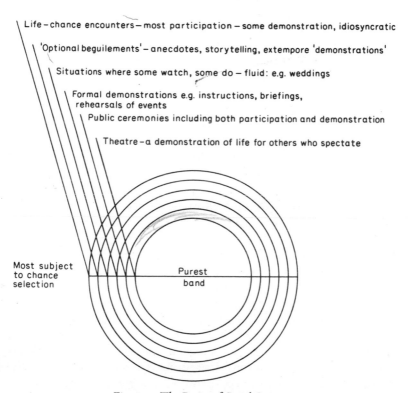

Life-chance encounters—most participation—some demonstration, idiosyncratic

'Optional beguilements'—anecdotes, storytelling, extempore 'demonstrations'

Situations where some watch, some do—fluid: e.g. weddings

Formal demonstrations e.g. instructions, briefings, rehearsals of events

Public ceremonies including both participation and demonstration

Theatre—a demonstration of life for others who spectate

Most subject to chance selection

Purest band

Figure 1. The Purity of Social Occasions

The point at which we move from being a participant in, to a spectator of an event is critical: as soon as there are 'those who do' and 'those who watch' the event, it begins to move towards the right hand side of the continuum. The actor is clearly at the extreme right hand, because for the time he is removed, by the theatre convention, from showing his own life. The lone individual in a private event is clearly at the extreme left hand, and spontaneously 'selects' behaviour which is fitting to his own reading of the situation. Goffman calls such occasions 'the least pure'. Theatrical presentations are 'most pure' in that the actors prepare an event for others to experience. If the audience do not come, there is really no sensible purpose in going ahead with the play. Within such a pure situation the actors have a different range of experience from the audience although both forms of experience are equally real: the actors and those who watch are both visiting other rooms consciously and productively; both are freed for the time being from the burden of the future and the chance elements of real life.[5]

There are many different blends of purity. Social events may be elaborately planned and be long awaited or they may arise spontaneously. They all reveal how we function as social animals trying to explain and make sense of the world.

It can be readily appreciated that one important aspect of experience which this 'other room' of Brecht allows us to see is the 'degree of selectivity' which different occasions require of us. The observer can see which kinds of behaviour have been selected. Those times when we can be observers help us enormously in those times when we must participate by providing a bank of stored information to be drawn upon. How 'pure' then is the occasion of a bedtime story or a raconteur telling a story at a bar? What of those times when we watch *and take part* – weddings, funerals, enrolments and passing-out ceremonies? What of times when one gives careful instructions to others? Is the purity of Hamlet saying, 'Speak the speech, I pray you,' akin to when a craftsman briefs an apprentice at work? And what of briefing before battle and meeting friends and asking, 'How was the interview?' One of the Goffman's beautiful terms for such spontaneous occasions as the latter is 'optional beguilement': a magnificent definition.

As a teacher I seek to keep people's experiences 'real', that is I try to bring about a change, a widening of perspective, in the life of the real person, as well as to offer systems of learning and knowing. I feel bound, therefore, to take account of Goffman's *Erving* notions because they seem to me, better than any others, to give meaning to the many blends and manifestations of drama activity.

FOUR FACES OF DRAMATIC ACTIVITY

I can find no basic conflict between those teachers who prefer to make and show plays to others and those who prefer to base their work on games. Between these two there are many subtle shades of activity. The learning which might come about is not really to do with the activities themselves. It is to do with the quality of the experience for the group and the relevance of the activities to the underlying purposes of the teacher. I have struggled to perfect techniques which allow my classes opportunities to *stumble upon authenticity* in their work and to be able both to experience and reflect upon their experience *at the same time:* simultaneously to understand their journey while being both the cause and the medium of the work. My techniques embrace all the ways which enable classes to do what seems important to me. In learning these enabling techniques, I have neglected others.

The four faces of dramatic activity which I can see are:

1. *Making plays for audiences*

This can be a meaningful experience for children, or adults, or for anyone doing it because they are interested, and not only because they wish to live in it and earn their money by it. Making plays seems to have gone out of fashion in education possibly because people did not learn to do it well with children who were not necessarily committed. When we ask this of children, we must treat them as the artists they can become. For too long in schools we have refused to let children function as artists. We make them learn *about* it.

2. *Knowing the craft, history and place of the theatre in our lives*

The study of the history of the theatre, of different styles of acting and playwriting in our own and other cultures is surely of great value. When they are placed in a sociological setting they stand with architecture and art: to help us to understand people in their cultural context. They help to reveal what all people and all cultures have, in their time, found to be significant.

3. *Learning through making plays*
This uses the *materials* and *conventions* of theatre to build upon the children's reflective energies: to limit the world to certain agreed aspects freeing them of the burden of the future; taking out some of the chance elements; being more selective in their responses and recognizing their reasons in doing all of this so that they may reflect upon what is changing in their perceptions of others and of themselves.

4. *Using the conventions of 'as if it were' to motivate study*
A great deal of my work is concerned with this because I see it as one of the principal ways in which schools could be humanized. It is using the conventions of the depicted world to motivate study of the real world and of humanity, providing a framework of purpose for and within the school curriculum.

These are all education. They are all exploration and allow children to function as artists and they all produce changes in perception. But their processes are different and demand different skills from the teacher/leader. Their basic materials are the same: people exploring their own attitudes, reflecting upon living and expressing their point of view as precisely as possible but realizing that it is a temporary moment of perception and may change *in the act of expression*.

It is impossible to contemplate all of this without running into the terrifying complexity of the word 'role': a complexity which is to do with the varying ways in which we function in different social situations under so many different kinds of authority and power. It is to do with the many levels of our existence within a vast range of social patterns and the many different meanings we make of how the world uses us and our personalities.

The word 'role' runs straight through Goffman's analysis. Our actor who is this night Hamlet is also at other times a father to his children, son to his parents, citizen of his country and so on. He is also an actor who is also a spectator. All of these aspects of role concern me as a teacher. The children are in role as students while I am placed in the role of teacher. But as a teacher when am I functioning as a director, as a playwright or as a counsellor?

Perhaps we might look for a different centre to drama as a way of learning, in order to find our way out of the drama/theatre abyss. So far we have tended to put the word 'artist' at the centre, without of course allowing children to function in that way. But should we meet in sociology? Should it be in psychology? Would the theatre see this as a true centre? If we embrace Goffman's idea of purity framings, we must make some attempt to clarify the centre to our different-seeming skills.

Brecht has really said all of this very succinctly indeed in his terms as a playwright.[6]

. . . I am a playwright. I show
What I have seen. In mankind's
                                    markets
I have seen how humanity is traded.
                                    That
I show, I, the playwright.

As a teacher I have to be selective too, helping people find frames of reference, understanding tension as an aid to learning.

How they step into each other's rooms
                                    with schemes
Or rubber truncheons, or with cash
How they stand on the streets and wait
How they lay traps for one another
Full of hope

This is the spectator in me, the sociologist who perceives the manifestations of people and their concerns. It is also the technician who perceives the means of the manifestation.

How they make appointments
How they hang each other
How they make love
How they safeguard the loot
How they eat
I show all that

As a teacher I cannot afford my own monitoring-out of what interests others. It is very easy to say that and very difficult to live up to affirming and valuing the ideas of others.

The words which they call to each
                                    other I report.
What the mother tells her son
What the undertaking asks of those it
                                    takes under,
What the wife replies to her husband.

The perennial watcher — the teacher's life-style, that of becoming con-cerned.

All the begging words, all the com-
                                manding,
The grovelling, the misleading,
The lying, the unknowing,
The winning, the wounding,
I report them all.

The psychologist and the sociologist, able to perceive, acknowledge and allow the reality and the humanity of social life.

I see the onset of snowstorms.
I see earthquakes rolling forward.
I see mountains in the middle of the
                                road,
And rivers I see breaking through their
                                banks.

The artist in the teacher accepting nature as a means of inventing new forms. One of my tasks is to fore-shadow for children the outcomes of their present acts.

But the snowstorms have hats on.
The earthquakes have money in their
                                wallets,
The mountains have arrived by motor
And the headlong rivers control the
                                police.

The artist/teacher translates and transforms easily from the seeming ordinary to the new view — the awesomeness of a new look, a new outer form for a universal inner meaning.

To learn how to show what I see
I turn up the representations of other
                peoples and other periods.
One or two pieces I have adapted
                                precisely
Testing the techniques of those times
                                and absorbing
That which is of use to me.

The struggle for form to communicate the ideas. The acknowledgment that we can borrow from those cleverer than ourselves.

I studied the representations of the
                great feudal figures
Through the English: of rich
                                individuals
Who saw the world as space for their
                freer development.

The recognition of the past as a model.

I studied the moralizing Spaniards,
The Indians, masters of delicate sen-
                              sations,
And the Chinese who represent the
                              family
And the many-coloured lives in the
                              cities.

The teacher as respecter of different ways of doing things.

There are three ingredients to my growth as a teacher:
1. To remain accepting of the ways and present conditions of others while considering how best to interfere, and that I seek to bring about shifting perspectives and understanding. This includes me as well as those I am responsible for.
2. To be able to affirm and receive from others.
3. To remain curious.
It is in the spirit of the accepter of what children bring to the situation — always the receiver, the curious one, the playwright, the creator of tensions and occasionally the director and the actor — that I have to function.

In Practice

THREE SESSIONS

Dorothy Heathcote worked with the children's group for three sessions. The over-all pattern of the work was as follows:

Session One
1. She asks the group about their attitudes to teachers and to drama.
2. They agree to let her choose a starting point for the work. She looks at them for a few moments and then speaks to them, in role, as the Captain of a sailing ship carrying pilgrims.
3. She establishes that there are sixteen pilgrims on board but only fourteen have paid for the trip.
4. Out of role she discusses with them some of the factual back-ground to pilgrimages to Jerusalem and the conditions on board the ships.
5. In role as Captain she hears the complaints of the passengers about the bad conditions of the voyage and long delay in leaving.

6. She leaves them alone to discuss the situation and then returns in role as a sailor.

7. The passengers try to persuade the sailor to arrange a mutiny. The sailor refuses saying he has no reason.

8. Out of role they discuss the work so far and decide to change the convention. They will explore the passing of 'the ordinary days' of the voyage. She asks them individually if they are travelling in 'hope or despair'.

9. In role as a grand-daughter to the pilgrims long after the voyage she asks them to describe what it was like and their reasons for going.

10. She asks them if, in the next session, they want to carry on working on this theme in this way.

Session Two

1. She compliments them on their involvment in the first session but says she is not sure what interests them as she doesn't really know them.

2. She notes down a number of suggestions for new material: they decide to look at 'watersheds in people's lives', e.g. weddings, funerals, divorce. They select funerals and want to look at the events before, during and after a particular burial. They also want to be free to develop their own relationship with the person and not all have to be relatives or debtors etc.

3. They decide to have somebody to represent the body in an open coffin. One of the boys volunteers.

4. She asks the group to arrange the space as a crematorium with the body on a blanket. In role as an undertaker she finalizes the arrangements for the ceremony: flowers, hymns. Much laughter between her and the group.

5. She tells them that mankind has always had to make arrangements for death and asks them what sort of service this is to be. They decide that it will be secular. The dead man was an ex-alcoholic and has requested that there be no alcoholic drinks and no unnecessary grief. It is to be a time of 'rejoicing'.

6. They establish that he had three wives. She meets the workers at the crematorium as one of the ex-wives and checks the arrangements.

7. After asking them if they are ready to go to the funeral she takes the role of the director of the funeral home. The group

become the guests. As they work within the situation she notes her observations on the blackboard.

8. They discuss the man and his work. He was an architect and designed his own coffin.

9. She asks them how they would like to develop the work in the next session. They are interested in 'the different strands of his life'.

Session Three

1. The funeral home is re-established. They discuss the life of the dead man and their relationship to him, individually.

2. She asks them to discuss in groups their part in his life, and his in theirs, together with their feelings towards him.

3. He lies in the centre of the space and she asks them to come to him individually, when they are ready and if they want to, to speak to him about any aspect of their relationship with him. She says that the convention can be altered for this.

4. She comments on the silence as they are waiting and asks if it bothers any of them. She asks if anyone wants to sing in the background 'to make it easier'. No-one offers so she says that she will sing although she can't sing well. She does so quietly.

5. The wives come to him separately and ask him why their marriages failed.

6. His parents also come to ask him about his attitudes to them and to his work.

7. A group of boys sit at the back by a table apparently uninvolved, talking amongst themselves. DH asks them who they are. They say that they were colleagues of the dead man in his business. They introduce the idea that he was involved in fraud partly to subsidize his drinking. Large sums of money are involved.

8. They come to him as a group and confront him with this.

9. They discuss the developments of the session and she thanks them for their involvement.

SESSION ONE IN DETAIL

The group sit in a circle facing DH who sits with her back to the audience. She says that schools are places where things should happen that make sense and have a meaning for people. She asks how many of the group feel that teachers are the 'tellers' who know what children do not know. A number of hands go up. One of the boys comments that teachers usually do know more than the children. She says that there are many things that she knows that they do not because she is older and has probably done more but there are many things that they know that no-one else does. For example, she has never been a man.

KR: Are you trying to establish here that the children have something to offer and that all the ideas will not be coming from you.

DH: Yes, but I'm also breaking the ties with the teacher's territory. I'm trying to get rid of the idea of the teacher as a 'special authority' person.

KR: You asked the group immediately after this to be aware of the audience not just as spectators but as participants in what was going to happen. In his sessions, Gavin asked the group to ignore the audience and asked the audience not to respond openly to anything the group did. Why this difference in approach?

DH: As I grow older I get more interested in *primary experience*. The audience are there. They do affect us and we might as well face up to it. Let's not be dazzled. What we'll find out is what happens to us when we know they're there. It's this primary need to accept all the factors in the situation.

KR: What did you see when you first sat down with the group?

DH: The first thing I always see is the lines of their bodies. But really what I see is what they are seeing when they look at me. Of course, I can only assume that what they see is an old lady because when you're fifteen anyone over twenty-five is ancient. But what I'm mainly tuning into is their sense of territory, how their eyes work. I quite deliberately put my back to the audience to confirm their nerves: that they've got something to be nervous about in front of this lot.

KR: During the course of this introduction are you thinking about what you're going to do and how to lead into it?

DH: No.

KR: When does that start?

DH: It starts when I feel that they've looked at me long enough to know whether or not they think they can get on with me. It's to do with sending out as many signals as possible of support, affirmation and also that I am me. One of the high tolerances I have is the 'you-ness' of you and the 'me-ness' of me.

She asks them if they do drama at school – they do – and what their expectations are. One of the girls says that drama is about social situations. Dorothy asks if they mind if she makes notes on the blackboard.

KR: Why did you write their comments down?

DH: In case the audience hadn't heard and also to let them see the total of what they'd said. I wanted to set out the terms in which we were going to be working together – to form a contract. After all they are not necessarily committed to this type of work as actors might be and this is a big difference.

KR: You ask them: 'Will you all participate with me?' Some of the audience commented later that you seemed to be giving the children a lot of choices but it often also seemed that you had decided in advance what you wanted them to agree to: that they weren't real decisions.

DH: Yes, I think that's what people would see demonstrated. After all they aren't party to the teacher's thinking. They were not false decisions. That would be lying. I do care for their decisions but it is not just a matter of what is said or tone of voice. It's all in the body and the physical attitude. When someone asked the children later if they felt forced to do things they said no. They felt free to do anything they wanted to do.

She asks the group if it is her problem to set the situation. They say it is. They are all happy with this. She asks: 'Are you giving me rights as a teacher, or passing the buck?' They laugh.

KR: What did you feel about their reaction?

DH: They were happy because what else could they be? It's easier to say yes. There's no point in fooling ourselves about it.

KR: Is it important then to ask the question?

DH: Yes, because I'm not only in the process of *now*. I'm in the process of laying down courtesy for a very long time. So when I say, 'Are we agreed?' I realize the unreality of the question. But the system I would not deviate from forever, is started and is going to go on. Only time will prove the value of it but to me it's ever so important. Insistent courtesy, insistent requests, insistent affirmation of people.

KR: Was your question about passing the buck serious?

DH: Most serious – to let them see that they can pass the buck but to ensure that they know that that's what they're doing.

She asks them if they prefer to go straight into the situation or sit and talk about it first. They prefer to sit and talk. She asks them if they have ever gone straight into the drama without discussing it and they say they haven't. She asks: 'Will you take a small chance with me and let me start one for a few seconds. Then we'll stop and ask, "Could this go on?" The danger is that as we are strangers if we discuss it we won't get anywhere.'

KR: If you felt this, why did you give them the decision in the first place?

DH: What I'm really saying is that, 'it seems to me that your experience is one-sided'. So I've really gone back to before I asked the question. I asked the question too early. We know that if they talk about it they'll never get into that thinking/feeling area that drama has to teach in. I don't really mind if they talk about it but I wanted to show them the other face of the card.

She asks them: 'Do you want a situation where you have a lot of power or one where you can live lives that you never dreamed you could live? Do you like going backward or forward in time.' One of the girls says that it can be 'any situation'. DH replies: 'I see. You're actually giving me free range to select from all human concerns. As long as it's interesting.' Laughter from the group and from the audience.

She asks them if they are prepared to 'take on strangeness'. They say that they are. DH: 'OK I'll fire an arrow into the air and we'll see . . . Are you happier starting standing up or just like this.' Just like this.

KR: Had you now seen a starting point?

DH: Yes. There was now some sense of territory and a reasonable relationship developing. 'Strangeness' is a vague word. It seemed to me to relate very well to their 'nowness' feeling of strange and to another interpretation of strange. It allowed maximum inter-pretation. The lesson is now entering a new phase. The first phase is finding out their expectations about teaching. This is most important.

Standing, she says to the group: 'I haven't got a plan for a situation. You'll have to take that on trust. I'm not lying. I think it would be very stupid of me to plan even a first science lesson before I had found out how people *think* about science, the nature of their knowledge and social interactions. I'm just going to walk around and see what there is here that starts something off in my mind. I believe the best drama always uses as much truth as possible.'

She walks away from the group and stands at a distance by some display boards facing them and the audience. She pauses and looks steadily at them. Finally she says: 'I see a group of people who seem in no hurry. So it can be a situation where there is time. I see a group of people who seem relaxed and they're facing inwards as if they belong together. They have said all there is to say. So I see a situation which is going to hold all of these and the only lie that is going to happen this morning is going to happen now.'

KR: Why did you walk away from them?

DH: Only so that they can see me from a long way off. So I can say in all honour what I saw in passing.

KR: What was the point of the last remark about the lie?

DH: Everything I've said to them so far is exactly what is there. They have said everything there is to say. They are relying on me. What I'm going to say now won't be true. I deliberately said 'lie'. It's a good way of getting them prepared. I think it's a word actors should pay more attention to. It's the magic 'if' when we're being fancy. It's the lie we're going to use.

She pauses and says to them: 'Are you gigglers when you're nervous? This often destroys work doesn't it. I respect why you giggle but I also believe you can control that. Will you accept a convention with me. When you feel a giggle coming on . . . don't catch an eye. This situation will involve maturation and self-control. So I understand but I've got a short toleration of it.' Laughter from group and audience. Changing tone she says: 'Tallyman! You said there were fourteen pilgrims on board. There are sixteen. Which two are new?'

DH: I mentioned the giggling because I saw a movement in one of the girls and I wanted to stop it spreading. I also wanted them to see that they can. I paused because I wanted them to see that my intention is now very serious. Secondly to fill the space with the idea that 'some things have got to happen sometimes'. And then I got baulked by a movement by one of the boys. I was thinking of something to do with *period* and so I got 'tallyman', I'm not particularly proud of tallyman but it was all I could do in six seconds. 'Tallyman' set it before steam. Then *numbers*. I didn't attack any individuals, I only dealt with them as 'its' so they didn't have to respond as individuals. I emphasized that the tallyman had given me the information because that gave the group some power over me and space to negotiate.

KR: The way you set the situation up initially will obviously have a crucial effect on the way the work develops. Are there any general criteria to which all your opening statements and strategies conform?

DH: Yes. I'm always concerned with their ideas about territory and the teacher. It is also important that they recognize that what is about to happen will take place by an act of their own will. There must be time to accept. The other one is that everything that happens must be significant. The amount of information you offer in any negotiation needs enormous precision. It's important in drama work to see a difference between *effective* and *affective* action. Effective action is what you do to others – it's obvious behaviour. Affective action is what you do to yourself; the quality of the thinking and feeling underlying effective action. I think there is often a broad difference between what people see in my work as compared with Gavin's, say. It is related to the evidence of cognitive and affective involvement by the children. This is mainly a matter of degree. You can read the cognitive more easily in Gavin's work and the affective more easily in mine because that's what I display. But my cognitive level is deep-hidden and Gavin's affective levels are often only limned in because he's less *demonstrative* in the affective and I'm less *demonstrative* in the cognitive. I feel my questions affectively with the class. I use space and body images, vocal power, and all of this hides my cognitive questions. It's just the other way with Gavin. It's sometimes difficult for people to see this when they watch me work because I'm apparently so busy filling the space with practical details.

KR: What do you mean when you say 'cognitive' and 'affective'.

DH: 'Cognitive' is my thinking process, my mind's knowledge. 'Affective' is to do with feeling and evaluation. My weakness is that I can't translate the affective 'language' of space and sensation into academic language forms. The danger with my work is that people may see it as blousy because they don't perceive the knife-mind underneath and this is important. The knife-mind is incisive.

KR: 'Cognitive' is sometimes taken to mean 'intellectual' processes in education and 'affective' to mean the emotions. In saying that drama is to do with affective education there is a danger that this will be understood to mean that drama and the arts are mainly to do with developing the emotions, and not so concerned with 'thinking'. How do you react to this?

DH: If the arts aren't to do with intellectual thinking then I don't see how you can have art because it must be given form. The two are there with all people and must be. But there is a value in these terms because of seeing the need for balance.

KR: In this session when you called to the tallyman, you had taken on a role to initiate the drama work. You didn't tell the group what the situation was and then ask them to get into role before you started. One of the main characteristics of your teaching is your use of role. Why do you use this technique?

DH: Because often my classes do not understand theatre. I don't always go into role. People think I never do anything else because they only see me *start* work. I often work with groups and don't go into role. It depends on the nature of the group and of the work. If I move into role, I put the emotive, the tension element, in immediately. I don't have to spend hours telling them that, 'if he does that and you do that it'll look better,' and all that nonsense that role can achieve in half a minute, because you are only asking them to *respond*. And this is so important. *Their responses have power.* I think it is utterly idiotic to ask them to do it all, initiate and respond. Would any art teacher say, 'I'm not going to give you anything but I'd like you to make some art'? Would anyone say, 'Play this instrument but I won't give you one'? But if they are only asked to respond to the violin, whether they think they can or not is immaterial, it's given into their hands so that they can find a response. And that's what role is. As soon as you move into role you are, at first, carrying most of the dramatic elements in order to introduce and affirm them: not to be copied but so as to make them understand that they can respond. They've got 'selectivity' in the work. They can stand up and move in space and then I can respond to their imagery and start *to become redundant*. If I introduce a more complex level of negotiation, like expecting anti-social classes to agree among themselves, they'll need me in role again.

In role, you're giving the group information on one level and throwing a challenge at them on another. Always you're trying to specify who, what, when, how, why? It involves setting tasks at the effective level to develop commitment at the affective level.

In the beginning I expect to negotiate very heavily in the overt task, to win commitment. I never anticipate high commitment. I always assume I may have to work at the lowest level of commitment and if this is so, by clearly specifying the task, I can at least win a modicum of co-operation. If I'm in role there's no losing 'honour' in obedience. If there is high commitment I make very few specifications about the task. The balance between task and commitment can be charted (see Figure 2).

In every negotiation I know exactly where I am on this graph. I always know every time I speak or move how much is helping them with tasks and how much is demanding their commitment. Knowing this helps me to pay very strict attention to their answers – in word or action – and to interpret their readiness for challenge or the need for more comfort. You can imagine yourself walking up and down this tightrope as the lesson proceeds.

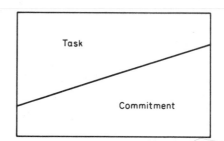

Figure 2. The Relationship of Task and Commitment in Drama Work.

Broadly speaking, the less able a class is at controlling social behaviour or where attitudes are negative the more I work to the left of the diagram. That is I specify task, individuality and how to start. If this group had needed it, I might have started the crusade situation thus:

Said	*Meaning*
Well, sirs and madams, allow me to greet you,	*Allowing sex separation but setting style: focusing on me and giving a pause before action.*
and welcome you aboard.	*Keep group together and indicate 'ship'.*
There will be a boarding charge.	*Warning in advance specifies money but not how much!*

Said	Meaning
I will be glad if you tender it as you board.	Money given is the leading action: as they step aboard is the subsidiary action (See p. 29).
A gold piece if you please, sir/madam. You will find space for your separate luggage below decks.	Now we set the period again and individual ritual. Every ritual must give each individual something to do after the ritual, while others are still going through it.

DH: As it was I was working towards the right hand side of the diagram and said instead:

Said	Meaning
Tallyman!	Sets period,
You said	not me, not class: another
there were fourteen	untrue
pilgrims	period, life-style, endeavour
on board.	ship
There are sixteen,	true – they can count if they like
which two are new?	definition of tension.

DH: I left all responses undefined because I had tested the group's attitudes and behaviour very thoroughly in the preceding negotiations.

KR: After you'd gone into role and introduced the idea of the tallyman, you paused. What did you see happening then in the group?

DH: I saw them wondering, 'What the hell's she on about?' There's usually a pause. You can't expect immediate take-up. There's nothing I can do at this point. I must wait at least a few seconds. They're thinking, 'Do we have to go along with this? Can we make any sense out of what she's saying?' One boy leaned forward and I thought he was going to say, 'Let's not.' So I thought, 'Right, let's hold.' Then at the last moment he looked around the group and they all followed his gaze. I'd been quite ready to say, 'I know this is silly isn't it. Let's try another.' That's why I said I'll fire an arrow.

She says to them: 'Now one of the things that has to happen in drama is that you have to get the sense of what the hell's going on. Do you get a sense of any particular time in period terms?' One of the girls suggests it is about the sixteenth century. Dorothy asks her where she got that from and the girl mentions *The Pilgrim's Progress*. She asks them if they got a feeling of ships. They say they have from the word 'aboard'. She then asks: 'Do you want me to go on with this a bit longer and see what happens?' They do. She asks them if they accept therefore that there were fourteen pilgrims and now there are sixteen. They do.

She says to them: 'OK, we have the only lie now that we need. We're aboard a ship and it's something to do with pilgrims. We don't know yet what kind because I haven't invented the characters.'

She says to them in role: 'I think I should explain that we shall not sail until all the dues are paid. Fourteen have paid their dues. Until the dues of the other two are paid there will be no sailing.' There is a pause. They look at her and wait. Finally she says to them: 'Now two things can happen now. One is I can do nothing . . . or I can help you do something.' They say they want some help. She turns to one of the groups and says: 'Where did you place your baggage?'

GIRL: On deck.

DH: So you did not hear the order to place everything below decks?

GIRL: No.

DH: That order was given late last night.

GIRL: I was sleeping.

DH: As I wakened every man and woman to tell them, I do not see how you could have been sleeping. Where is your baggage? Go and fetch it. Do you need an escort? Who knows this woman?

GIRL 2: I do.

DH: Tallyman! One bundle only may come down. See they bring it.

DH: In saying that only fourteen had paid I was setting up a tension which is crucial. I was also establishing conventions of choice: letting them know what the alternatives were for working inside and outside the drama. I began to individualize their responsibilities at this point to help them feel that they belong in the work and that they're not just a gang.

KR: When you'd said that there would be no sailing you stopped being the Captain and left them to it. Why was that?

DH: I must do, you see. I've got to do two things. I've got to win the drama but I've also got to win *honour* and that's the most important. It doesn't matter what happens to the drama if the honour's all right because we can do things to get the drama again. But if I make one false move on honour, I haven't really got anything. I have to throw thin silken lines across to them and however thin, they must be pure and honourable. All this is affirmation of the *thou-ness* of the children and I don't see how you can ever get learning of the type I want without honour.

KR: What do you mean by 'honour'.

DH: I mean that, 'Nothing I have done, whatever it has done, you need hide from me and I am not hiding anything from you.' Actually I am hiding my thought processes because I cannot show them *and* my negotiations at the same time. Equally they cannot show their thought processes. We're both less than the work in the long run but the honour is to do with making them feel secure – that I won't let them down. In most of what goes on in schools, kids feel dishonour and so I do tend to plaster with a big trowel. But it's not a façade. They're going to have to accept it if anything worthwhile is going to happen for them.

She offers a piece of gold for anyone who will say who the second person is and a boy promptly points to someone. She asks him where his baggage is. He doesn't know. She comes out of role and says that they're not sure yet where this will take them. She summarizes where they have got to: 'This lady hasn't heard a command . . . so she might be one of those two people. This man, to earn a piece of gold has told that another man is the second person.' She asks the girl if she is prepared to take on the responsibility of being one of the stowaways. She is but the boy is not. She turns to the girl who agrees that she has brought someone else on board but she will not say who it is or why she cannot say.

DH: Now that's interesting. Let's think of some of the reasons why a woman cannot say. . . . She could be being blackmailed couldn't she?'

GIRL: She may not want to betray a friend.

DH: I'm trying to show them here the implications of what they are doing. I must create reflective participation. If I don't do that, I'm not in art of any kind and I'm not in learning. Also I want to show that in any situation there's a mesh of interests. I'm trying to focus

in on a truly theatrical and dramatic mood. You can best consider
big themes by narrowing the situation right down. You can't do a
useful play about pilgrims, but you can do it about this woman's
choice and then it can become a play about pilgrims.

She asks one of the boys to give her his dues. He says he paid
the tallyman a few days ago. She says the tallyman wasn't there
then. She calls to the tallyman and then says to the group, out of
role, 'Of course we've got an interesting thing here, because we
have a non-existent tallyman who's very real for me.'

KR: Why did you contradict what the boy had said?
DH: His real signal to me was, 'Now then, I'm clever.' I threw the
same back because he was out of the drama when he was most
seemingly in it. He was really saying, 'Go on deal with that,
mate.' I mentioned the non-existence of the tallyman to show that
I could be lost as well. It was really a soother.

She asks them if they'd like to be left alone for a while. She
leaves them saying: 'OK I'll just go and see the tallyman for a
bit.' After a few moments she returns, asking them if they want
to talk about the reasons for the journey and if they want to
provide the reasons for it themselves or hear 'my framing for it'.
They want to hear her reasons. She agrees to tell them providing
they will agree to take decisions, when they want to, about what
is happening.

    She describes the visits of the pilgrims to Jerusalem and the
hardships they suffered at the hands of the boat-owners who
exploited them *en route* and overcrowded the boats.

DH: I did this because we'd had this farce about non-existent tallymen
and the word pilgrim had been dropped in once or twice. I won't
do drama if I can't at some stage help people to realize that all
dramas are celebrations of events that have occurred. I did it to
underline that, although we were simulating, such things had
actually happened.
KR: Why do you use the word 'celebration'.
DH: Because that's what I believe art is. It celebrates true significance
and I want children to be aware of the responsibility of this. I see it
happening in all drama work, although I wouldn't always say it to
all children. I wouldn't say it to six-year olds but I might say, 'But
shepherds do lose their lambs don't they?' By 'celebration' I mean
'to bring into significant recognition'. Nothing is insignificant

because we perceive and acknowledge it. That to me is celebration.

She asks them if they are happy to go on and tells them that they can go forward or backwards in time in the drama: 'We only have to find a meaning'.

KR: In his book *Personal Knowledge*[7], Michael Polanyi distinguishes between *focal* and *subsidiary* awareness in acts of perception and in our actions. He illustrates this by saying that if you are driving a nail with a hammer, you are aware of all kinds of sensations in your arm and hand and this is necessary if you're going to perform the task. But you are only aware of them subsidiarily. The focus of your attention is on the nail and the act of hitting it. I think this is useful thinking about the different levels of perception in drama work. I've seen many lessons where the focus of the group's attention is on the external actions of the play and they are only aware, subsidiarily, that it may mean something. You seem to be trying to reverse this here, so that the group's attention is focused on the meaning of their actions and they are only subsidiarily concerned with the actions and practicalities of the drama. In Polanyi's example, if the focus of your attention shifts onto the sensations in your hand or on to the hammer you miss the nail.

DH: Exactly. They must focus on the meaning of the drama and then the subsidiary actions will come right and true.

She comes to the group as the captain of the ship and says that she understands there have been some complaints.

DH: What have you to complain about? Your berths are comfortable are they not?

B 1: No.

DH: You've caused trouble from the day you appeared on this boat and now I understand you've rung me again. What's wrong with things?

B 1: The food's disgusting.

DH: The food's the best I can get you.

G 1: We've been waiting here a month and we've not moved.

G 2: It smells in here a bit.

DH: The boat is not yet full.

G 1: The blankets are flea-ridden.

G 3: There are rats on the floor.

G 2: We can't sleep at night.

DH: Sleep ashore.

G 2: I've paid to go on a pilgrimage. ... I want to know why aren't we going?

DH: We're not going because there are still more pilgrims expected.

G 2: Well get them.

DH: I cannot get them. My task is to be here in harbour when they arrive.

G 3: Surely you have enough money by now.

DH: Enough money? Money is not the point. I have to wait for those weary pilgrims who require my ship.

G 2: If money is not the point, why are you charging us?

DH: Because I'm paying men to wait on the tide and I'm keeping this ship seaworthy.

G 2: Seaworthy! You're joking. It's filthy.

DH: Filthy is nothing to do with seaworthy. As far as filth goes, who is making the filth. ... It was clean when you came aboard.

G 2: We've paid to go on a pilgrimage.

DH: I am paid to take you to the next harbour.

G 2: Well take us then!

DH: I cannot take you until the boat is full! ...

G 3: It won't take long to take us to the next harbour. You can always come back for the next pilgrims.

G 2: They will wait for you.

G 3: I'd wait after we've travelled all the way across France. It's very important to us.

DH: I appreciate your troubles. I appreciate them.

G 3: If they appreciated the trip they'd be here on time wouldn't they?

DH: I believe there has been quite deep snow. ... I'm doing what I can. I have issued more of these blankets that you are so critical of. Why do you not travel with all your needs?

G 3: There's a lot of holes in the blankets.

DH: That is not my problem. The blankets were provided and they were good. ... Ladies and gentlemen, if you are not happy with the ship, go and seek another.

SEVERAL: We've paid for it!

DH: Of course you've paid. The choice is yours. You can wait until the boat is full or you can go and seek other harbourage and other ships.

G 3: How do we know the boat will ever be full?

DH: The boat will be full.

G 2: When?

DH: When the boat *is* full! How can the boat be full until the boat be full?

G 1: Can't you be more specific about that? . . .

G 2: The boat will never be full.

DH: The boat has always been full before. . . . Do not place on me all those matters that are your affairs. Seek your God, Ladies and Gentlemen. *Uproar. She walks away.*

DH (out of role): Do you think you can manage for a few minutes by yourselves?

SEVERAL (quietly): Yes.

DH: Now, the trick on this one is don't start acting your socks off, and carrying on. . . . What will we see? What will happen? And there's always two kinds of happening: the things that happen outside to you and the things that happen inside to you. OK? Now what I'm going to do is withdraw and I'll just keep on dealing with the ship for a bit. The point at which you want me back, will you just indicate? . . . But indicate when you come and fetch me whether it's Mrs Heathcote you want or the Captain and that way I'll stay within the drama or within the tools, you know.

KR: What were you looking for from the group during your questions and responses here?

DH: I wanted to allow them to grumble but to specify what was wrong and get committed to 'pilgrimage' and the life-style and problems of pilgrims. I decided to step out because while I was there the situation stayed with 'attitudes'. When I leave they may hurry the plot. I made the comment about acting their socks off because I wanted to see if they would fall into the trap of only developing the plot line.

She leaves them, as the Captain, suggesting that they clean their quarters. They begin to blame the girl, who was sixteenth, for the problems and accuse her of being a fraud. One of the girls suddenly asks in role, 'Why are we arguing among ourselves. We've got to sort our *our* problem.' DH then re-enters in role as a sailor.

DH (whispering): Have you seen the Captain? (Some laughter in the group.) I've taken three trips over. It's always the same. . . .

I've seen the ship set sail so deep down in the water going across we've been lucky to get across.

G 1: What can we do?

DH: She is a sound ship. You'll be all right. I'm just telling you. You're hanging on here but you've got a month at least I would say.

G 1: A month?

DH: It will go . . . and what's more he'll bring you back. Some of them won't even bring you back.

B 4: What, for more money?

DH: Well of course, you'll have to pay.

G 3: What if we haven't got any more money?

DH: Look lady, I don't know. In fact, I says to meself, why in hell do you do it?

G 3: Why didn't you tell us before?

DH: I haven't been in a position to tell you before. He ain't been off for a while . . . he's gone into town . . . for supplies and that.

SEVERAL: Supplies! (*Uproar*) What for!

DH: Well. To feed you.

G 2: We'll have to pay I suppose.

DH: Well OK. But he's buying in the market like all the others you know.

G 3: Isn't there anything you can do?

DH: Look lady, I'm just a sailor here. All I do is, I know about ropes and sails.

G 1: Why can't you arrange a mutiny? He must be . . .

DH: I ain't arranging no mutiny.

(*Shouts of frustration*)

G 1: I mean he gets twice as much as most of the men in this ship get. I mean you can just split the money between you, can't you?

DH: I don't want the responsibility. I'm all right.

G 2: You're all right but we're not. You have no consideration for us . . .

DH: Look don't argue. You've only got a month.

G 1: Well we've got to decide what to do haven't we?

DH: I agree.

G 2: We haven't got any money.

DH: Have you paid all your money?

G 3: Every penny of it.

DH: Come off it, you must have some more put aside.

G 3: But only enough for food.

B 5: What are we going to do when we get to Jerusalem?

DH: Well, I've never been to the Holy City. All I do, you see, is go from coast to coast.

G 2: You go from coast to coast and you've never seen the Holy City?

DH: What reason would I have for going?

G 3: Don't you believe? How ungodly.

G 1: How can you live your life without actually seeing it?

DH: I haven't got the time. I'm only a sailor. I can't be going to the Holy City.

G 1: Yes you can.

G 2: It doesn't cost you a penny to get there.

DH: Well, why are you so worried because you haven't got no money? . . .

(*Some quiet laughter in the group*)

G 5: Would you call yourself a good Christian man?

G 2: How can he be?

DH: I obey the commandments. I don't envy nobody. I haven't committed adultery yet.

SEVERAL: You steal though. You steal . . .

DH: I don't steal, lady.

G 3: You've taken our money.

B 2: It's the Captain who does that.

G 2: But they get it back from him. That's why they don't want to arrange a mutiny.

(*Pause*)

G 3: If you were a bit more hard on your Captain, he wouldn't be so hard on us.

DH: If I was hard on my Captain, I wouldn't have nowhere to lay my head, nor yet money to keep my family. Thou shalt not steal saith the Lord. . . . I think you're just going round in rings in your minds. That's what I think.

G 1: What else have we got to do?

DH: I don't know.

G 5: No, I agree. She's right. We've got to do something more positive.

G 2: What can we do though?

G 2: Why don't you give us some of the food you eat. I've seen sailors looking fat and drunk.

DH: I know, I know. They get bored an' all.

G 1: Bored! With all the money they've got?

B 2: They don't even sleep on board.

G 2: They get bored with doing nothing. They're supposed to be sailors. They're supposed to be sailing not doing nothing.

G 4: If you're bored, why don't you clean up the ship. That'd be something to do.

DH: I'm cleaning up the ship in my way. I can't clean up the rubbish you left. I'm looking after the caulking of this vessel and this vessel is well caulked.

DH: What have the others been doing?

DH: There'll be no holes between the planks on this ship. The other sailors have been doing what they have to do. But I noticed when one of them was sick, the other week, there was nobody down there saying a nice little prayer or anything.

G 1: We didn't know he was sick or we would have helped . . .

G 2: Why was the sailor sick anyway?

B 4: Too much drinking.

DH: No, they say it was a kind of heartbreak. . . . He got a piece of paper. I don't know what it was. Some kind of heartbreak.

G 2: So he was sick in fact. What do you think we ought to be feeling like? We've been waiting so long and we're waiting to go to the Holy City.

DH: I can tell what you're feeling like, madam. It's written all over you. . . . I'm just trying to help.

G 1: Well try to help in a more positive way.

DH (out of role): Right. You're beginning to sound like argumentative pilgrims now. Is that how you're feeling.

SEVERAL: Yes.

KR: Why did you decide to come in as a sailor?

DH: The sailor role could deepen 'pilgrim' rather than 'grumbler'. I could also deepen the tension and the danger by giving inside information – what the Captain could 'hide'. I choose the roles I do because I know precisely what each role has gained and can gain and so I know what is yet to be gained and make a role – or another device – to service that. All through this section they slowly believed more and the 'spectator' was lulled while the 'participant' in them built a belief. There is real proof that we can play the games of our clever parleying, without destroying the idea of the crusade. Spectators became fully present towards the end of this.

KR: It's interesting that when you are in role they sometimes refer to you as 'she' and sometimes as 'he'. When one of the girls agreed with you as the sailor she said, '*She's* right'. How do you think they are seeing you when you're in role?

DH: I exist for them in two dimensions. Mrs Heathcote *is* 'she'. Mrs Heathcote/the Captain *suggests* 'he'. They are in Brecht's two rooms. Both are real, though one is depicted.

She tells them that they have got hold of some kind of reality in the voyage now but, because it's a drama it doesn't have to stay at this level. She says: 'What we have at the moment is a simulation of how it might have been when a group of pilgrims were waiting, frustrated. . . . Your very faith is perhaps being eroded as well. But in a drama we can do anything we like. We could go back to find why you came or we can hurry forward to the next outcome. We can say, 'All right, the voyage is over now and we are leaving the ship.' . . . We can find you as effigies on tombs and learn of the lives you had. What sort of ideas do you fancy now. . . . Should it be in a crisis – what happens to the pilgrims? Or should it be how the ordinary days pass?

G 3: The ordinary days.

DH: . . . You've chosen a very interesting area. Have you all chosen it? Some have said it but others are going along by default. . . . If you choose the ordinary days then we have to find a way of passing a lot of ordinary days without taking everyone inexorably through every second. Do you see what I mean? So we need a new convention.

KR: Why did you encourage them to change the convention?

DH: I think that children, like this, should be able to experience and be offered a large variety of conventions. This group didn't really need to stay in a simulation like the crusade situation. A simulation is when, like life, you live through a situation, not knowing what the outcome will be. This is OK but there is a lot more to drama and learning than that.

The group sit in the same shape as she says quietly, as background: 'The bird that flies above the ship, his eyes can see those who need to be alone and those who need yet to be together. The bird does not know what is in the minds of these people. . . . 'Tis the bird that sees the men and women bound to the ship and the journey through life and who listens to the souls of these people and looks into their eyes. Would the bird understand these faces? And the bird who knows about this food and the seeking of his own food, what would he know when the great dish is brought up? Grub up!'

She places 'a bowl' of food down. The group begin to complain about the quality of the food and to say that they cannot stand this anymore. She stops them and says that although everything they say rings true: 'You're tending to take the top layer of your mind and of course it always works easier if you can complain. . . . But now will you take the second layer of your mind? When I bring the soup, I'll just put it down. Don't say the complaints. They are there. . . . We've got to remember that in the twentieth century our palates are much changed. A lot of the food the people would eat then out of necessity, we'd throw away. But now . . . I'm asking your minds to work rather differently but still stay pilgrims . . . I know you can grumble, but allowing for that . . . let's take another layer. Is it that we now feel bound together or is it that now the life of the spirit is important? . . . But what you talk about is in all these other areas except grumbling. OK? There you are. Caught yesterday.

G 1: Well, we've got to eat something. If we don't eat that today, it'll be served up to us again tomorrow.

DH (as background): The bird who seeks his own food – what do these men and woman seek?

G 1: Does anyone want any biscuits?

DH: They say that the spirit of God belongs to all people. But I see still that there are those who grab and those who wait. (*Pause*)

G 1: I suppose to the Captain we're just like all those fish in the sea. Just a bunch of nothings, anonymities.

G 4: We've been out about a week now.

G 1: It seems like about a year. The days are so long.

G 3: What are we going to do when we get there? . . .

G 4: The sailors said they'd bring us back.

DH: Are you sure?

G 3: We'll probably have to work our way back knowing the Captain.

B 2: We'll take a coach then.

DH: That's interesting. Did you mean a coach with wooden wheels?

B 2: Yes.

DH: Yes. You see, he's speaking from the innocence isn't he, that

he's brought his own culture, his own life, to this situation and if
there are coaches where he has come from and if he's living in the
sort of society where he can pay, then he'll expect, you know,
'Bring us a coach.' . . . Probably the land is very different. I think
we could guarantee some kind of transport on legs that you could
afford to hire. . . . Let's take the next step. I'm very impressed
with the way you're letting yourselves be gradually taken further
along on the journey of the pilgrim. It's a matter of finding the
reality of it for yourselves. . . . Imagine packing. . . . Everything
has got to be carried over quite a long period of time. There are
the sorts of things you might *need* to take. Then there are all of
those things that you take because . . . you would not be *you* if
they were not there. At different stages in life the things you
cannot leave behind change. And then there are the things that
we carry for our comfort – to keep you well and healthy.

She asks them to find a space where they are not near anybody else. She insists on this saying that, 'some of you are
blocking each other because you need to rely on each other a
bit'. She asks them to begin to place in three bundles the different
things they need for the voyage. When they get up she asks them
to move in a way which helps them feel that they are 'out of
time'. She asks them to try and feel 'the spirit of all men who
place their homes upon their backs and walk'.
    As they move about she says in the background: 'There is a
place for watching pilgrims and there is a place that is home and
each person must find that place out of time. When in this place
the ship recedes, timeless, and men truly find what they are
looking for.'
    She pauses and asks each of them in turn: 'When you look at
what you are, is it in hope or despair?' Several reply on either
side.

KR: What are you trying for here by changing the convention?
DH: To see if they can be individuals and still believe in the pilgrimage
    without either the support of arguing with a role or each other. I
    am not in role here. This is a watershed. *I am asking them to under-
    stand a universal.* So I am a commentator and out of time.

She asks them now to try and make another transition: from 'it is
happening now,' to 'one day I will try to explain this to somebody.' She says 'If you survive Jerusalem you will tell your

grandchildren of this time. Keep the reality moving forward and talk the memories ... all talk to yourselves, no-one will hear anybody.'

After a few moments she says to them that she is going to ask them the same question twice and it is going to be asked a long time in the future. In role she asks, 'What was it like Granny when you went to Jerusalem? What was it like Grandad? You went to Jerusalem.' There is a silence. She says: 'Trust yourselves to explain it to me.'

DH: You went to Jerusalem. What was it like? Can I go there? Will you take me, Granny? What was it like?

—: I felt Jesus there.

DH: What was it like on the ship, Granny? (*Pause*)

—: It was all right.

DH: They say you had horses. Did you see them? Could you ride them?

—: No it was too crowded.

DH: Was it very crowded? What did you do, Grandad? Why did you go? Why did you all go? Why did you go, Granny? Will I go?

—: If you want to.

DH: How do you know when you want to go to Jerusalem?

—: ... When you want to find peace of mind.

DH: Did you find it?

—: Yes.

DH: All the time? What's peace of mind, Granny? ... Was (Jesus) there?

—: No, but you can feel him in your heart.

DH: Why did you go, Grandad? Granny says it's inside you.

—: You wouldn't understand. You're too small.

DH: They always say that to me. I'm twelve! ... Was it worth it?

—: Yes.

DH: Why?

—: Because Jerusalem is more where Jesus was and it makes you feel closer to him.

—: You find out who you really are.

DH: But I know who I am.

—: Well, you find out why you're here.

DH: But I know why I'm here. I'm going to be a knight.

—: You can't be a knight.

DH: I can too. Everbody can be a knight if they want to.
—: Oh come on.
DH: You mean if you want to be something you can only find out what people will let you be, not what you want to be?
—: No.
—: It's not a very nice thing being a knight.
DH: Well, why do they get all the honour?
—: Wait and see when you're older.
DH: Everyone says wait and see. Do we have to wait? . . . It seems so long waiting to see.
—: The longer you wait, the more it seems worth it.
DH: They all say that.
—: You'll be saying it when you're older. You'll understand then.

She stops them there and leads them back onto the boat as pilgrims and asks them as themselves where they see the play going next. She points out how they might be changed by the journey and the problems of having to return to a mundane existence after such an experience. She says to them: 'This seems to be a constantly recurring theme for all of us doesn't it? You go away and you come back changed, not necessarily by the Holy City but by the actual experience of having been there.'

She asks them if they want to move into different themes in the next session with different conventions, or perhaps even work on a new idea altogether.

End of Session

KR: Why did you choose to take the role of a grandchild in the closing sequence?
DH: To have been their children, at my obvious middle age, would have been ridiculous and the idea of 'child' might have awakened embarrassment regarding sexuality in so public a situation. So I chose grandchildren which was a straight reversal of our ages and removed the idea of them having had the children themselves. When I first asked them to reflect on the journey there was silence, so I asked them in role to enable them to reply. I think that one of my life's perfect teaching moments lies in their responses to me during that sequence. And some of the onlookers called it a performance! the memory of the event seemed a good way to bring the crusade to a close because I changed the convention. But it did not prevent it being continued if they so wished. I drew

them round the board at the end to see if they could now do what, at first, they could not have been expected to do.

KR: What had the session achieved?

DH: When I meet a new group, it is essential that we deal honestly with each other. This means recognizing *everything* in the situation and dealing with it. When I am called 'teacher' and the others 'students' there are questions of power to be dealt with in terms of their expectations, built up over a long time in schools. I have to provide 'comfort' without betraying my own goals which is to give power away. Some classes can't believe this and so at first I may have to take the power they expect one to take. Also, because I am a teacher and I have chosen to work through drama, I have to awaken both the participant and the spectator in each member of the class. When the two are present, we can learn and participate in the art form. All my negotiations in this session were either creating comfort so that they could participate; creating reflection on the events so that they could take more power and make choices about the next events and the content of them; or providing forms in which they could find expression of their ideas until they could create their own forms.

All of this was done through minute negotiations: choice of words, spaces, style of language, tone of voice, pace of delivery, types of phrase, facial expressions, body signals and territoriality. It is difficult for observers, watching from the outside, to perceive this as the class did, being at the receiving end. Most observers view from doubt, which preserves them, or too admiringly, which leaves them too vulnerable. The rare observer who can set opinion aside and say, 'What is happening here', will more clearly perceive the inner structure and affect of negotiations with a class.

Broadly speaking, all the preliminary business of the crusading ship was providing comfort. First the group of waiting people able to argue. You can always find your tongue if you can argue with someone or grumble and I gave them plenty to grumble about. Then the ordinary seaman who could help them to widen their areas of reference about their plight. The Captain gave them a position from which to argue but the sailor challenged them to think more seriously about what they were doing in the boat. But the Captain was important for the participant. The inaction of being on the ship was their comfort. They need do nothing unless they so wished. It may seem that I had all of this planned. Of course I did not. How could I know in advance what type of comfort they would need? I only needed to use the playwright's understanding of tension to select quickly what seemed an appropriate setting for the occasion.

KR: Is it true that you never plan a lesson until you know the group or would you sometimes have a situation in mind before meeting a new class?

DH: I might. If I've taken a brief from a school I might know very clearly. If I've gone in to teach *Julius Caesar* I would know precisely the area I wish to get into and the strategy I'm going to use. What I wouldn't know is how they're going to walk with me. So I'm very clear on what, in that case, but not how. One never ever uses old settings. They are chosen uniquely for each event and each group.

When they believed enough in the ship – and this was brought about as much by my interruptions out of role as by the Captain and the Sailor – it was easy to shift to the memory of the crusade. I never intended that we should simulate a crusade only that we should make a metaphor and find ourselves able to participate in it.

I ended the session with the chance of change because I knew that the crusade was only my choice of a starting vehicle. It did not represent their interests but it served to get something begun. But what was begun was not a play nor yet an improvisation. It was the start of trust and a honourable relationship in which we all took risks and did not let each other or the drama down. Now the real matters had a chance to begin.

KR: What was your thinking in approaching the subsequent sessions?

DH: At the end of the first session they had shown that they were prepared to try out ideas even if it meant leaning on mine to begin with. They had treated each other's ideas with courtesy and those who had led in the talking did not seem to object to carrying the others. When I offered them the chance to change from the pilgrim theme I did not think they would change just for the sake of it. I wrote their suggestions on the board so that they could all see what they added up to. I never mind what suggestions people make. As soon as I can see the implications of their suggestions – in the words they choose and the manner in which they give and take ideas from each other – I can begin to sort out what really interests them. I can then put all my energy into finding a form in which their ideas can find a first expression until they find forms which suit them better.

I think some people felt that I knew all along what form I was going to use. But if I *want* to push an idea there is nothing to stop me doing so *openly*. After all they can only refuse. As I watched their suggestions come on to the board, I began to classify them and saw these main themes: drink, experiments with relationships, working life, and male/female contacts.

I tried not to force a quick selection but there is a 'feeling of failure' to be considered. If I let them not choose for too long some may lose heart and that can quickly spread. They had already used one form which they hadn't chosen and I didn't want to choose the next one for them, even using their suggestions. I wanted to let them choose so that they felt they were getting somewhere. As soon as there was any kind of selection I said, 'Let's start and set it up.'

It seemed to me that my invention of a convention would help them to free their ideas. Notions for drama at first are often cloaked in a kind of web of unperceived ideas which gradually work themselves free as the work progresses. I spent some time thinking of a convention which would comfort them now into these newer regions which are closer to their own interests than the distant crusades. When I came back to the studio after the break I read a comment to the effect that we haven't come here to watch Dorothy Heathcote showing off. After all my thinking this was a bit of a slap in the eye! But it was only to be expected if the writer looked from the outside of the work. Some of the group who were waiting asked me what I had thought up for them and I mentioned the idea of a funeral at which we could select our own ideas for airing. The boy who later became the corpse asked me quietly if he could be the dead man. I said yes and I know why he asked. If you are used to plays being simulations, you expect corpses to lie down and be quiet! But the selection of this convention allowed the group to deal with whatever they wanted to for as short a time as they wished. The corpse convention was a comfort factor. It forced relationships to develop but not to be acted out. They could talk about all of those ideas on the board without having to expose themselves to the onlookers in any action.

The three sessions ended with what I felt to be the start of a relationship where the group and I could experiment with anything we felt like trying. I don't think it would have mattered whether it looked like theatricals, improvised drama or dance. We had the start of a very exciting partnership.

Work with the actors

Dorothy was invited to work for one session with the actors' group. It was a session which caused some controversy at the conference. It took place on the final day.

The general pattern of the session was as follows:

1. She sits at a table in the main studio, the actors on chairs facing her. At either side of the area, and facing the audience, are two blackboards. Two members of the conference, one an actor, the other a teacher, have been asked by Dorothy to comment on the session as it goes along and to describe what they see. They give their comments to assistants who write them on the blackboards. These are transcribed by a third assistant on to a long roll of paper as a complete record, the boards being cleaned regularly as they fill up.

2. She says to the actors and the audience that she wants to set up a situation where 'some of my thinking and some of the actors' thinking can be seen'. She will set up a situation where the actors have performed a play in a school and have been invited by the head to discuss ways of following the work up.

3. She chooses the story of Jason and the Argonauts and tells the story in outline.

4. In role as headmistress she thanks the company for having worked in the school and speaks about ways of using the material in the classroom. The two 'universal themes' of mental health and the nature of being a hero are mentioned as being implied in the story.

5. The actors settle with her on the general theme of 'what keeps us sane under stress'.

6. As headmistress she talks about the nature of education and of teaching.

7. She asks for one of the actors to take the part of Jason and he puts on some costume to suggest a cloak and helmet. She arranges him as a statue and discusses with the others the details of his posture and the impression he conveys of his state of mind.

8. Other characters – Medea etc. – are cast and positioned in detail.

9. As the end of the session approaches the actors are sitting down in directed positions – 'universal postures' – in preparation for a group of children whom they might be meeting in the class-

room. Each actor is given a line to say which comments on his/her character and attitude. If the children were to ask them initially what is the matter with them they are to say, 'It is our leader.'

End of Session

KR: One of the striking features of this session, and one which caused most controversy, was the extent to which you talked about drama and what the actors *might* do if they went into a school, but how little they actually did do in this session apart from listen. Many people felt that you has mis-used the actors. What were you trying to achieve?

DH: This session was really for the benefit of the audience rather than of the actors, as compared with the children's sessions where the emphasis was on the value of the work for the group. I had thought a lot about this session in planning for it. Looking back I think I made my usual mistake, that of assuming that people will suspend their doubts while they examine what is happening. I had four things in mind in planning for this.

1. Actors rightly come into schools with the results of their ideas and work already established.

2. Teachers, as teachers, don't necessarily understand at all that actors have been trying to do in playing in schools. The gap is in their intentions. This is a dangerous gap. I have seen many distressed teachers sorting out children after an actors' visit. And at the same time actors have often had to suffer enormously because of a lack of understanding of their needs, by the school, when playing a play. We can all think of examples.

3. I had introduced Goffman's notions at the beginning of the conference and I thought, because people seemed sympathetic to them, that I had been understood.

4. The teachers I know would often love to have further contact with an acting company after the performance. Often, for many reasons, they can't, not the least of which are the rigidity of the school timetable and the financial pressures on actors themselves, compelling them to cover as many places as possible.

It seems to me that we have had little time to thoroughly investigate how teachers and actors can enter a partnership in using drama and their different professional skills to enable learning. I set up the situation in which they could choose which aspect of a role they had previously performed – in a play which we can assume would have had a plot and narrative developments – and which they could develop and use for teaching. I wanted, above all, to show the internal thinking of a teacher. That is why I set up the recorders at each side of the room. I felt it would be important for all of us to get unguarded responses from the two professional disciplines we had set out to explore. I could have provided comfort in these areas and looking back, I might say I should have done. But I watched the actors with Bill Gaskill and they seemed flexible up to a point and to have open minds about teachers. I merely limned in those aspects of teachers which can appear fulsome to visitors who come in to schools for short times.

KR: The comments which were written on the two boards varied a great deal from the actor to the teacher. It seemed as if they were watching very different processes. Where the teacher was writing, for example, 'Creating significance' or 'Looking for the universal', the actor was putting down things like, 'They are waiting to be cast.' Someone commented: 'It was interesting to note that the teacher's blackboard at no point recorded the actors' unease but was busy recording Mrs Heathcote's good intentions.'

DH: There were points when they agreed and disagreed but this is the main area in which we don't bother to communicate. It was important to show this because if we can't find a common point of view then we have to start at the beginning and I think that is where we are. You can't have actors working in schools if they don't examine the nature of teaching and the teachers' perceptions of them.

KR: Some people felt that you had blocked the actors' energies and that you had misused them: that you were 'domineering and patronizing.'

DH: Yes I felt that reaction coming across. May I pose a few questions?
1. Does it seriously matter that on one occasion talented people are blocked a little? I was trying to do something I have rarely had the opportunity to do before: to use actors in role in the classroom and introduce them to the interior of *my* teaching mind, which is the only one I know.
2. Were we looking for conclusive ideas, or tentative ones, or explorations of potential development?
3. When three people are invited to develop their own work in an open way with onlookers present, are they supposed to confirm

everybody's preconceptions, or affirm future choice or to challenge thinking? Should they present an 'old act' they know to be safe in that it offends no-one, or should they be exploratory?

The teacher must work very rigorously in planning for the growth of children's perceptions. Mostly there is not the necessary rigour in preparing for learning through drama. In trying to show this to the actors I of course blocked out their usual ways of working out their ideas. The resulting fury was there for all to see. Nevertheless the picture I painted of rigorous preparation for the use of role in the classroom is a true one. Ironically, one of the Royal Shakespeare Company had seen such a role shortly before the conference and said that it demanded far more rigour than their evening performances because it relied for its life on the interchange between the role and the class. We are not in the inner circle of purity any longer!

Postscript

Thinking back over the work and discussions of the Riverside Conference it is possible to define some areas which might be given more thought in the future. I raised some of these points in my opening statement but I realize that although they may be applauded in words, in practice they may be more offensive than at first they might have seemed. They are equally important and all suggest the need for further exploration.

1. I asked the actors if they felt that I had 'violated' or 'aborted' their art during our session. They thought that these were overstatements. But it was clear that both had been felt. We are concerned here not with one person's teaching style but with a very important challenge to schools and to actors. In what ways can theatre people work to bring change to educational settings?

2. Gerald Chapman hopes that young people will be 'given a voice' in his theatre work. In this respect the theatre may be ahead of most schooling. What are the different ways in which schools and theatres can generate and support young people's emerging ideas and feelings? The teacher often 'tacks' in the nautical sense so that, although the outer activity constantly

seems to change direction, the over-all inner direction of the work is the same. What is aborted for teachers when actors do a play in school? What is aborted for actors when teachers use roles to 'tack' about?

3. How far can theatre and schools, by approaching one another, make a safer journey possible for pupils through the differing pressures of subjects, aims and explanations of intent offered in the name of education? How far can theatre share with schools' drama the task of enabling learning?

4. We must explore the watershed between experiences which bring a moment of discovery for oneself, and the experiences of demonstrating those moments for others. In Goffman's analysis of role, it is clear that this demonstration aspect does not belong to the theatre alone. At what point does a funeral service cross the bridge from being an experience in itself to being a demonstration for others? What then of this drift between that which we realize and that which we show and communicate. In the course of teaching, the teacher is crossing the chasm in both directions constantly, sometimes every few seconds.

There are four aspects of dramatic power within this discussion for which we must develop a language of explanation and communication (see Figure 3).

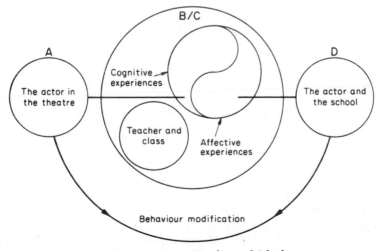

Figure 3. Actors, Teachers and Schools

A: At Riverside we saw actors seeking to awaken their resources and to communicate their ideas to onlookers. At one level there is the subtle alchemy of generating ideas and their implications for the actor as creator. At another there is the craftsmanship of communicating in space and time: creaking joints slowly giving way to balance and equilibrium.

B/C: In the work with the children, elements of theatre-craft were perceivable: the teacher working to provoke and gather the ideas, energy and interactions of the class and helping to shape those ideas into meaning. Whether the cognitive is in the ascendency – where we clearly see the teacher's mind at work – or the affective – where the outer form is broad and may seem unsubtle – in either case the intention is to enable the class to stumble upon moments of authenticity; enabling them to move forward in the depicted world of the drama while feeling unthreatened in their real relationship with the teacher.

I saw the same moments of authenticity during Bill Gaskill's work. Each teacher will blend these cognitive and affective pressures according to their comfort, instinct and aims. Both are required in whatever mix by both teachers and theatre directors. In teaching the children it is apparent that two skills are present simultaneously: the skill of the playwright to create and define the tension and the skill of the actor to apply and demonstrate it so that the classes can catch it.

At this point in the diagram the actor and teacher cannot share common aims neither can they help each other. But they do share common tools: body and verbal language styles; skills of analysis and of generating and focusing tension and the outer manifestations they employ to make meanings and awaken response.

D: For some time actors and teachers have been experimenting with ways in which actors can move in the teachers' world of helping children in the 'negotiation of meaning'. It is here that there are most opportunities for immediate development and it was this that I wanted to explore in working with the actors.

In theatre the actor works within a framework of ideas developed by the playwright and in performance moves something like a vessel under full sail through well-charted seas. If they venture into the classroom as participants in teaching, their function and power is different. They are more like ships with sails limp, ready to be filled by whatever breath and strength of wind the class blows in their direction. They give a focus to the class's energy. It is the children's perceptions of them which will fill the sails and create and direct the voyage they make.

At first sight this may seem like a travesty of theatre art, but it is the crucible for experiment and the discovery of new forms – forms which I believe are now ready to be explored.

I was recently working with a class of deaf adolescents on ideas coming out of an 'O' Level Religious Studies course. Their teachers were concerned that each time the group was introduced to new concepts the children had a tendency to make the sign for 'rubbish'. Each child was partnered by an adult who took on the role of a stone-age person. The task of the adult was to respond to the child's handling of the situation and in particular to create opportunities to make these 'rubbish' signs back in response to new ideas: for example, when the child taught how to make fire or chop down a tree or turn a stick and stone into a machete. But making the sign had to encourage the child to work harder on the explanation and not function as a derisive rejection.

In some ways the actors are working here as in the theatre. They are building belief in the depicted world but also being pushed in new directions and to explore new sub-texts which emerge from the particular needs of the class.

We might take as a final example a group of actors performing *The Crucible* to an examination class and then the actors playing John Proctor, Elizabeth and Abigail working with another class on ideas of marriage and responsibility. It is essential in this case that the children do not just feel that they are 'meeting some actors who know more about this than we do', but that the actors in their dealings with the class both in and out of role are able to release the power of the class to deal with this dilemma. The sub-text – what is really happening here? – will develop as the teacher brings together the acting roles and the hesitant class who do not yet know their capacity to deal with such problems.

It may be argued that actors are not required for such work, that they are stunted by it, that it is of no value for them. It seems to me however, in his work with the actors, that Bill Gaskill was doing something very akin to how they would be called upon to create in the classroom. If a dialogue is to develop, if theatre people wish to involve themselves in education – in giving children a voice – here is one of the most fruitful areas to till and explore.

If educators will not shift schooling into using more balanced cognitive and affective teaching styles, here is an area where the work of sensitive actors could begin the process of moving our schools into the twentieth century. But it will not happen purely by bringing theatre into schools as performances for the schools, nor if they continue to plan their interactions between players and audience shabbily. There is a mine of treasured contacts to be won here through patient, rigorous and sensitive experiment.

What could happen, the relation of class/school to theatre

2. Working With Actors

Bill Gaskill

When I first went into the theatre there was weekly rep mainly, and some reps were lucky enough to have three and four weeks rehearsal. In that time there were golden rules – like don't bump into the furniture and piss off down left – and there was never any concept of *exploration* of anything other than the presentation of the text through very fixed rehearsal patterns. Now you know what happened in the theatre: subsidy grew, rehearsal periods became longer (in some theatres) and suddenly we were confronted with the possibility of starting to think in terms of those great theatres in Europe – like the Moscow Arts, like the Berliner Ensemble – where they had apparently unlimited time to explore the material of the writer and to refine the performance.

We didn't really have the equipment to cope with it, because the theatre in this country has been, and is still to some extent, anti-theoretical. We'd *heard* about the Method which was practised in America – which was a version of a Russian's method – and we'd *heard* about the Epic Theatre of Bertolt Brecht, but these were alien forces. Some of us tried to come to terms with what they meant in practice and it wasn't easy because, although we read all the theory, we still didn't understand what the practice was. In fact, I don't think I really understood Stanislavsky until I read a book, written by somebody else,[1] which actually described what he did, day by day, in rehearsal and then I understood what it was all about. But up till then, from the books of theory alone, I hadn't understood. I certainly didn't understand about Brecht from reading his theories until I saw the work of the Berliner Ensemble. Then, having seen the results, we had to back-track into finding how, by what means, what methods, those wonderful results were achieved.

But, more important, while this was happening, a new school of writing was beginning in this country and it really wasn't paying much attention to the theories of Brecht or Stanislavsky. The writers were writing the plays they wanted to write and we had to direct them as they were written. So we tried, sometimes, to impose what were so-called 'Brechtian' methods on to writers who manifestly rejected them. But on the whole we went with the writer as the prime-mover. And that's still basically the position that I'm in as a creative artist and I think, generally, it's the position of the theatre as a whole.

There was a strong and vigorous influence of work from America which was basically non-verbal, which came via Grotowski, a Pole, and through very impressive American companies who had a lot of influence on what we now call Fringe Theatre. But, interestingly enough, a lot of that work, I would say, has disappeared and has been largely replaced by Political Theatre in a way which is certainly indigenous to this country. Drama took on itself the responsibility of making political statements. Now that is something which came from us here and not from the outside at all. In fact there is, I think, very little Political Theatre of that kind in the States and precious little in Poland either. Simultaneously there was that vast outpouring of work, in some senses very strongly separate from the work of Traditional Theatre: the enormous outburst of Theatre in Education; the whole development of touring groups and community theatres: all work more closely related to the needs of the community; to work in schools; to work mainly outside London.

A lot of it is not writer-dominated. A lot of the impulse for the work comes from the actors or the teachers because there is now a tremendous overlap between teaching and the actual presentation of dramatic work. As I understand it, 'drama' in schools does not now mean what I would have meant by drama at one time – the whole body of written material which has been handed down to us from the past – but the performance or improvisation of non-written material.

I think this has set up a situation which has a potential which is not always fulfilled. I don't know quite where I stand myself. I have used quite a lot of improvisation in rehearsal and then again

I haven't. I tend to adapt what I do to the situation in which I find myself: for example, the length of rehearsal time; whether it's a West End Show; a show at one of the large subsidized theatres or a show with a Fringe group, as they're called. Each one has different needs and the end product, and its commercial demands, is also going to influence my rehearsal methods and how much teaching I actually do.

Directors are funny animals. We are half teachers and half conductors. Some of the time you just work as a conductor with people who are extremely skilled, who know their jobs through and through, and your business is just to orchestrate, control and let them work through the pattern of the writer's work. Sometimes you are directly training an actor while rehearsing him. because drama schools are very inadequate in training and don't adapt quickly enough to the needs of new and experimental theatre. They are always training people ten years behind the times so they don't sense the values of what's happening in the living theatre and therefore don't find the right training methods and they lack flexibility. That's very important, I think. Flexibility in practice is what it's all about.

Sometimes I've tried to impose methods. I did say to Edith Evans once: 'Dame Edith, we will be doing some improvising in this production.' And she said: 'Improvising? Is that what William Poel would have called "paraphrase"?' So I said: 'Yes, I think it probably is.' And it was, that's the amazing thing. Poel[2] probably understood that what he was aiming for was to get her basic understanding of the text through a method which was not all that different from what we would mean by improvisation. She never actually *did* improvise, to my great sorrow: I mean, I never actually got her to do it.

The nub of the work, I think, is at what point you try to free the methods of work so that it has some value for the theatre as a whole. The other thing is that in the process of the changes we've been through, the actor has become a much more independent, analytical and critical person than he or she ever was before. I think that's been a tremendous achievement. Because actors have had to take new responsibilities – for the running of groups, for the creation of plays – in the process they have learnt a kind of independence which can only be healthy, and I think it's in that area I am most interested: how you get the actor to think for himself and to make decisions about his own work in relation to a text, in relation to the work of everyone else but to consciously assess, criticize and evaluate.

In practice

The general structure of Bill Gaskill's three sessions with the actors was as follows:

Session One
1. He says that he wants to work in 'observation and memory'. He asks the actors to give details of their own backgrounds.
2. He asks one of the actresses to take a specific memory from childhood and to set this up as the basis of an improvisation. This is repeated several times with questions from WG.
3. One of the actors is asked for another situation: one where he felt humiliated. This is enacted. WG asks for it to be repeated several times to show different attitudes on the part of certain characters.
4. The audience are invited to comment on what they see.
5. A third actor is asked for an incident from childhood. WG asks for specific details of the incident. The group enact it. It concerns a teacher beating a boy in a classroom. WG asks the actors what they think the scene is about and then invites the audience to comment.
6. There is a discussion between WG and the audience about the reasons for/morality of, the teacher's action.

Session Two
1. WG reviews the first session for the new audience. The actors repeat the classroom scene. The audience is asked to comment. They criticize the teacher's attitudes and comment on the implications of his actions.
2. WG asks the actors to repeat the scene and directs 'the teacher' to be 'more sympathetic'. The audience are asked to comment. They see no difference in the two versions.
3. Scene is repeated a third time. Audience discussion with WG about the problems of teaching and discipline. He asks them to stop interpreting and looking for implications: they should

consider the incident objectively, 'whatever subjective areas there are'.

4. Fourth actor is asked for a new situation. He tells of an incident at college with his girlfriend where he became jealous. They run through the scene.

5. Discussion between WG and audience about his aims in doing this.

6. He asks the actors to leave the room and decide on a scene and then to play it to the audience without telling them the story first. They do so: brief incident between a mother and her young daughter asking for her first bra: 'Don't be silly dear. You haven't got anything to put in it.'

7. They are asked to do another. They come back and enact a presentation ceremony in front of a school for a retiring teacher who goes on to make a racist speech: 'You black children and I have had our differences but I know that under your black skins you're as white as the rest of us.'

8. Discussion between WG and audience about the moral responsibility of the headmistress and other staff who sit on the platform during this and, although deploring her attitude, do not comment.

9. Scene repeated to bring out the reactions of the other staff.

10. Audience discussion with WG and actors.

Session Three

1. WG says he wants more activity from the actors and less involvement from the audience. He wants now to switch from childhood memories to 'more specific situations'. He asks the actors for 'a time when you made a personal decision to become involved in an issue when you would have felt guilty not to be involved but in getting involved you had to decide when to stop'.

2. Actress recalls working in an exclusive shop: in the tearoom a member of the staff starts a bigoted discussion about immigrants. Should she get involved in the argument?

3. She is asked to cast the scene and they go through it. She does not play herself. The group feels that the scene lacks clarity. It is repeated – she plays herself this time. It still lacks clarity.

4. Another incident is suggested: one of the actors was sitting in a bar when a group of black people came in. The barman starts to make jokes about them obviously expecting him to sympathize with his attitudes.

5. The scene is enacted several times with casting changes. They feel that the scene as a whole has not worked but that individual performances were good. WG says that he is mainly concerned 'with the reality of the scene'.

6. Actress tells a story about exorcism which leads to a general discussion about mysticism and the occult, religion and superstition. WG says that he is 'completely unmystical'. He doesn't want to see the scene but asks each member of the company if they can give a monologue on some aspect of mysticism.

7. One of the actors tells a story about a Hare Krishna girl. During discussion of this WG says he is not clear about the details and asks him to explain it differently. Actor asks: 'Do you mean in a Brechtian sense.' WG asks him what he means by that. Actor says he is not sure and this develops into a discussion about the dangers of theory and using jargon.

SESSION ONE IN DETAIL

The audience sit in a horseshoe shape: the actors sit at the open end facing them. WG sits with the audience directly facing the actors. He says that he isn't sure what he's going to do but that he wants to work on observation and memory.

KR: Why did you sit with the audience?

WG: I often work like that. I must relate directly to the actors. I must sit facing them as I would if I were directing them in a play and they must respond to me. In a normal rehearsal I stand for the audience anyway, which is why the director sits, in a proscenium theatre, facing his actors. When I teach, I try and keep that relationship. If I have to explain anything to the audience who are watching it with me then I turn around and try and involve them so that they feel a kind of identity with me working. But I don't want anything to come between the actors and me.

KR: When you first sat down, did you have any idea at all of what the pattern of the session was going to be?

WG: No. I work very off the cuff as a teacher. I like to have a starting idea – what I'm going to do in the first few minutes – or I panic completely. But after that I like to respond very much to what happens and – though I think I did this too much in this session – to respond to reactions in the audience watching.

He begins by asking the actors to introduce themselves. He starts by giving a brief account of his own social background and life. One actor begins: 'My name is . . . .' WG interrupts: 'No. Can you give us a bit of background.' Actor starts to give details of his career. WG: 'No. Can we have something a bit more grass roots? What was your childhood like?' Two of the group go on to give general curriculum vitae, mentioning academic qualifications etc. Three give general accounts as asked for.

KR: In a drama session with children, or in work with non-professional actors, the leader or the teacher usually has to work, in the initial stages, on welding the individuals into a working group. Does the director have a general role of this type for the actors?

WG: If you put a group of professional actors together they become a group almost immediately. You can't actually stop them becoming a group. You can do exercises to make them relate to each other but an acting group tends towards homogeneity. You know, they're all actors and it's their job to act.

KR: So when you're working with a new group to put on a show from a script, do you go straight to the script?

WG: No, not necessarily. You may do work, or discussion work, on the scenes of the script so that you find out how they relate individually and as a group, to the material they're going to work on. I've found it quite valuable to do that – not to spend a lot of time doing it. When I was doing *Madras House*, for instance, I used to start each of the sessions with the role of women in society and how it had changed since the play was written and explore what they thought, particularly the women. In the process you can't stop actors talking about their private lives, how many illegitimate children they've had. It's in the nature of actors to talk about themselves.

One of the things which obviously isn't so true with children is that the status levels in the theatre – the star levels – are such that, if you start rehearsing straight away without any kind of group activity, you may find your leading actors immediately removed and so on down the scale. Whereas, if you do something which everybody talks a bit about – their own lives or their attitudes to a subject – they level out, at least for that time. They have a sense of having an identity in the group. I do think that's very important, particularly in a big theatre company where you're playing a tiny part and you never have your voice. If you sit in a circle and they all in turn say something, then by the very fact of that they all have a kind of equality which I think is very important. It's not a true social equality but it oils the wheels.

Asking them for background information was quite deliberate because this was a group I'd never worked with before except for one. Originally I was going to work with *Joint Stock*, then I decided, rather arbitrarily, that that was unfair: that I ought to work with people I didn't know so I would actually have to come to terms with that group without relying on a lot of those common signals that you share when you've worked with people a lot. I'd met all of them before, individually, and asked them if they wanted do it but it was the first time we'd met as a group and the first time most of them had met each other, I think.

One of the actresses is asked for a specific memory from child-hood. She tells of an incident when, as a little girl, she visited her mother who was teaching younger children. The children didn't think that her mother was old enough to have a child of her own and thought that the little girl was her mother's sister.

WG asks her to set up an improvisation based on this, 'in how-ever tiny detail.' They enact the scene with her playing her mother. WG asks her if that is how she remembered the incident. She says it was not and when asked why she remembers it says that her mother thought it was funny and it has been told many times in the family, but she can't remember any details of the incident.

KR: Why was it important to set this up in detail?
WG: To remember it as precisely and accurately as possible and not to worry that it was not a dramatic moment but just to remember exactly what happened.
KR: Did you know before the session started that you were going to ask them to take incidents from childhood as the basis for improvisations?
WG: I may have done. I think I had been doing some work on observation and memory. When you choose something that they know, you have that, which is the supposed reality, and their relationship with it and immediately you've got material to work on.
KR: So far as you know were they all used, individually, to working in improvisation?
WG: Quite a few of them I would say. About half and half.

KR: But you obviously felt that they could handle this?

WG: Well you can never say that because whenever I've taught, even with people who've done many, many improvisations, they always say, 'Well we haven't done *that* before' and often, because there are so many different kinds of improvisation, I usually find with people who are new to me that the work I do is new to them.

KR: What was the general purpose of getting them to do this rather than, say, working from a text?

WG: I think I just wanted to do something that I thought I wanted to do, which is very typical of the way I work. I think it would have been good to work on a text but then I'd have had to have had the actors together for some preliminary work.

KR: One of the group said later that they were all feeling very awkward at that stage in the session because they were being watched.

WG: Yes, and they didn't know me and so there is a whole kind of lubricating process in the beginning. Often when you work with a new group they're a bit stiff. You have to get to know them and for the first moment of that to be under scrutiny is very strange. I'm usually rather tense anyway in the first stages of any rehearsal or session with a new group. But you also get some charge from it: you get a lot of excitement from demonstrating in front of an audience.

KR: Were you hoping that the actors would get something from the work as well as the audience who were watching a demonstration?

WG: It's very difficult to say that really, you know, because it is demonstration teaching. When you do demonstration teaching you are very aware that that's what you're doing and that you are being watched. It makes a complete difference. I don't think that I could truthfully demonstrate what I would do if there weren't an audience there because there *is* an audience there and it obviously changes the situation. I think this is very important in teaching. Every situation is *that* situation with *those* people. I wish sometimes that I could work as if no-one were there but you can't. You find that in a rehearsal room if, for instance, a few people come in and watch while you're rehearsing, it actually affects what happens. It certainly affects the actors.

WG asks the group to repeat the actors scene and to try and pinpoint what the eleven year old felt as a result of the children's reactions. They do so but the repeats seem to be identical and do not develop the situation. WG stops it and says that what the incident lacks is 'a moment of realization'.

KR: What were you trying for here?

WG: I was trying to find an angle or a handle to start working from. I mean, anything is interesting up to a point: any material is valuable but some things reveal more than others. Some you can take off on eventually. Probably there wasn't much there: there wasn't much dramatic yield to it.

KR: What do you mean by a 'moment of realization'?

WG: A moment in which the person understood or felt something. I don't mean at a very specific level. The improvisation was rather generalized and it should be like 'held-frame'. You should be able to say 'that was the moment that was vivid to me and the rest of the incident surrounds it'. It's like when you're analysing a scene in a play. You say sometimes, 'What moment does the scene hang around? Where is the moment in which the scene is most focused? What was the moment when you actually understood what was going on?'

In observation exercises I usually set it so that you don't play yourself. They play the person they've observed and someone else plays them. In this instance Jessie played her mother.

KR: Isn't that very close to a basic principle of psychodrama? In a psychodrama session, individuals are asked to take on the part of others in significant events in their own lives and re-enact them. Presumably you see a different function in what you're doing to work in psychodrama which is intended to be therapeutic. You're trying to get people to pinpoint the details of incidents and to reconstruct them accurately.

WG: Only as a starting point. As it goes on you start to show people in their social roles rather than in their psychological or emotional roles. They have to see, even in an emotional situation, the social factors involved, and that usually takes a lot of questioning and answering too.

KR: One of the intentions in psychodrama is to bring about a discharge of emotional tension which may be behind the memory of an incident.

WG: Nothing could be further from my thoughts. But it is interesting because it does lie in the same area which is what annoyed a lot of people, because I was using similar methods to quite different ends.

WG: Were you interested in the actress's emotional reaction to the situation?

WG: Not at all. Well, only in so far as she would then recognize it as being emotional but not in any sense for her to go through any kind of experience other than a rational one.

KR: But often the only reason we remember events is because they do have an emotional significance for us.

WG: Yes, very often. But if you do the exercise it's better to deal with things which are emotional so that they can be looked at objectively. I mean what's the point in looking objectively at something which you already know in that way?

WG asks one of the actors for 'the incident you can remember when you were most humiliated'. He remembers an occasion when his mother and little sister were laughing at him for something he'd done. In embarassment he stepped backwards and trod on his little sister's pot. WG asks them to set this up.

WG: I was pushing much more here. I wanted something which was vivid.

KR: One of the group said later that until this point she had been very nervous and guessed that the others were too. She felt that you weren't sure why you were doing this, and the feeling that you were groping towards something gave them little to hang on to. She felt much more secure as they began to set this up: 'Now I had something to do.'

WG: I think this is fair comment.

They play the incident. The mother and child say nothing but laugh manically. The actor comments that the actor playing him showed his feelings too openly. The scene is repeated. WG asks him if it was 'truthful'. He says that it was but felt sure that his mother had said something to him. WG asks him what he wanted to show in the story.

KR: Was this adding an extra layer to the work? You didn't ask this the first time.

WG: Yes.

KR: Did you want them to point it more as a performance?

WG: No. When you get them to try and analyse it's because what they want to show in the story isn't always conscious when they tell the story and when they think about it they don't always come up with the right answer but they try. Like he might have wanted to show that he hated his mother, you know. He didn't actually and there was a lot of analysis about his mother's laughter not in fact being cruel. It's very difficult to get that right so that it didn't look like an awful sadistic moment. It wasn't that at all. It was an accident.

KR: Did you want them to show why it was significant?

WG: No, I don't remember thinking that at all. I don't think 'significance' came in to it.

WG asks him if it would have affected him for better or for worse if his mother had hit him. They repeat the scene this time 'in order to show the mother's injustice'.

WG: This wasn't to show that the mother *was* unjust. But one way of testing what you *want* to show is to say, 'let's do the thing to *show* the mother was unjust even though that probably wasn't true.' Because then you can start to test what it was actually the scene showed or what he wanted to show. If you take a more extreme point you can level it out afterwards.

WG asks the actors to select individually a specific intention as characters and play the scene showing it. After they run the scene he turns to the audience and asks them: 'What was it they wanted to show us?' A number of interpretations are offered. Someone suggests that if they heard more about what had happened later they would understand more about this incident and the relationships involved. WG says that what happened later is immaterial: 'They are concerned with now, not later. The point is to reconstruct what happened and to see it objectively.'

KR: Would it have been immaterial if they'd asked to know more about that happened beforehand?

WG: Yes, really. I mean you only know what you know from what you've seen. That's one of the things of theatre. You choose what you show. You can't show everything. That's wonderful if the incident is expressive. You know what you know from that.

WG: Is that quite the same thing? The meaning an incident has for those involved is often to do with the network of relationships they've built up before the events take place.

WG: You can't show those. You can only show them through the moment itself. Where would you stop going back?   The marvellous thing about the theatre is that you say, 'I'm going to show you this moment in time'. So you look at that moment in

time and it's amazing how much you know backwards and for-
wards if you choose the right moment. You assess what you can
from that which is why the choice is so important. The action
itself is what is important, and from that you deduce psychological factors. But if you start with the psychological factors you
end up with a mess. The mother wasn't sadistic. The whole
temptation was to make the mother a monster but is simply wasn't
true. His memory wasn't that his mother has treated him badly
but the memory was vivid to him. He felt terrible but it wasn't
the mother's intention to make him feel awful. I'm sure he doesn't
resent his mother, he just remembered the moment.

KR: Why did you ask the audience to comment?

WG: Because the actor has to know whether what he has set out to do is
communicated.

KR: How did you feel when the audience continued to comment
throughout the session. This irritated some of the actors.

WG: Well, they talked too much but you try to be fair to everyone. In
the last session I was much sharper with them. If you're not careful you enter into a dialogue with the audience and the actors are
left sitting there not doing anything. It's very important not to
bore the actors for too long. It's a constant pressure because if they
get bored their energy drops. It's very difficult to get in a situation
where you have so much confidence that you just let things float.
It can be achieved in a very extended rehearsal period. I've never
been very good at that. I think some directors are. Brook knows
very well how to let things just happen. But that's a particular
kind of work and not one I've been very much into. I find when I
do dialectical work, which to some extent this was, or analytical
work, that the very fact of being watched by an audience is an
advantage because the actors are made to think and have to be
clear for the audience watching them.

The actors repeat the scene. The actor complains that it has
become their scene and it is really about him. WG comments:
'Of course, it's based on your vivid memory but as we flesh it out
it becomes more and more objective: it becomes more and more
like an objective view, one a stranger might see.' He says that the
actresses were better because they played with more subtlety and
did not suggest malice.

WG: One of the aims of the exercise is to be fair. What I'm
trying to do is to move from the subjective to the objective.

The audience are asked to comment on the scene.

AUD: I didn't feel a moment there that the actor would have remembered for twenty years.

WG: It doesn't have to be theatrical.

AUD: I'm not talking about theatricality in the sense of some big close up of him at some meaningful point. I mean it didn't feel important to the actor.

WG: It doesn't have to be. It has to be important to the audience.

AUD: But if it's important for him won't it be important for us?

WG: No.

Another member of the audience objects that the actor's own involvement in this incident has been disregarded. He offered to share an experience and now it has been monopolized by the rest.

WG: I don't want to share in his humiliation. I can't think of anything worse. This work is nothing to do with psychodrama or any of that rubbish.

He asks for someone else in the group to offer an incident. One of the actors tells of a time when he was at school. The teacher comes in and calls for quiet. He turns to the blackboard and as he does so, the actor remembers making a squeaking noise, just for fun. The teacher turns and demands to know who made the noise. No reply. Another boy has a smile on his face and the teacher accuses him of making the noise. He takes him to the front of the class to beat him with a slipper. The class protests that it wasn't him. The teacher, in some doubt, calls for the guilty party to stand up and take the punishment. The actor recalls that he had been scrumping the night before and didn't dare take a beating across the backside with a stomach full of green, raw apples.

The teacher threatens that if the guilty party does not own up he will assume the guilt of the boy he's picked out and beat him anyway. The actor remembers making to stand-up but being pulled down by a friend sitting next to him. The teacher says he will give the boy six strokes of the slipper. He does so. The boy cries and so does the real culprit – from guilt. For weeks following he bribes the boy with sweets during playtime to atone.

Some details of the scene are discussed and the actors set it up. The actor blocks the scene and they run through it with him playing himself. WG asks the actors what they thought the scene was about: 'The humiliation of letting someone else take the can.' 'The education system makes teachers very petty.'

WG asks the audience if they thought the scene was about the actor's choice.

AUD: It's a play about having no choice.

WG: Why no choice?

AUD: The teacher is trapped.

WG: No, he's not.

AUD: Teacher's like that don't exist. Should we concentrate on the teacher's moment of decision?

WG: If you think that's the point of the scene.

There is considerable disagreement among the audience about whether or not the teacher was right to act as he did: 'Should he be allowed to teach?'

Some members of the audience are openly annoyed at the way teachers are represented.

WG: But this is what he *did!*

Audience continues to raise questions: 'Wasn't he forced into doing this?', 'Who was the weakest?', 'Should he have hit him?', 'Do you have to carry out threats?'

End of Session

KR: Throughout this and the next session the audience spent a lot of time discussing the implications of the events they were shown. You tried to stop them by asking them to be objective.

WG: The difficulty is that you have to train people to see things. You know: 'I mustn't interpret, I mustn't interpret. I must just look at it, see what I get from it and not fit it into my ready-made plans. Just look at it again and see whether if what I think is really true.' ... At one time one of my obsessive exercises was to say, 'What happens? What happens? What happens?' And people would tell me and I would say, 'No, no. What happens?' And it became a kind of discipline to look at it in that way. 'Don't talk about "the universal", what happened? What actually happened? Don't make a comment on it, don't tell me what you think it means, don't tell me its symbolism, don't tell me what you'd like it to be. Tell me what happened.'

KR: What are you expecting of people when you ask them to be 'objective'?

WG: I suppose just not to see things from inside their own heads but to try and see themselves from the outside; to have some sense of themselves usually in a social situation, which of course I deal in a lot; to become aware that their values, opinions, judgments are conditioned; to reach that kind of self-awareness by actually scrutinizing their actions as if they were being performed. . . . What I want to explore is the actors' moral attitude to the people they present and the group's attitudes to the situations they present, particularly when incidents have actually happened which are factually based, where there is an historic objective truth. I'm interested in moving from a subjective approach to an objective one and in presenting a scene objectively in order that the social, political and moral factors within the incident can be assessed, so as to make the actors more aware of the social situation in which they exist. . . . It doesn't matter whether the teacher in the classroom scenario is neurotic, bad-tempered or whatever. What matters is that he's a teacher because it's being a teacher which gives him the power to beat the boy. If he weren't a teacher – or if he were in most countries – he'd be booked for assault.

When an actor performs someone else's actions then he's not necessarily trying to be objective but he is at least presenting someone else. When he presents himself, the effort of objectivity is very great. People know what you mean when it happens. You just strip off layers of subjectivity. You make them *think* about what they do rather than put up with their first, immediate, emotional responses. I work on the basis that people can think and I don't see why they can't think in the arts. . . . I don't see why the arts, why acting has to be a non-thinking profession. I don't see it.

KR: Gavin and Dorothy talk about working deliberately at 'the implication level', and looking for 'the universal'. As teachers they are concerned with getting children to think about the wider implications of specific events and situations; with using events symbolically to say much more than the events say by themselves. Would you disagree that the theatre uses events symbolically?

WG: Symbols tend to come about by themselves. This is a very basic difference because I do believe in specifics. That may be reductivist but the tendency, certainly in actors, is to lay too easily symbolic or emotional interpretations which it may not bear.

KR: But the implications of a play – its meaning – often go beyond the events which are enacted in real time on the stage. Isn't this intentionally so?

WG: But you can lay yourself open to whatever you want it to stand for. It can mean anything you like. I mean, *Othello* is about a black man. He's not a white man. The Merchant of Venice is a Jew.

You can draw parallels and say Jews are badly treated and so have negroes been and there is some resemblance between them but you have to be specific about that. What's the point if it becomes a generalized thing about avarice, say.

KR: So, when you start work on a text such as *The Merchant of Venice*, is your main preoccupation to bring those characters to life – to make their actions believable and plausible?

WG: No, not at all. You have to know what the play is saying and how it says it. . . . It very much depends what art you're working in and what branch of that art. When you paint a rose, you paint a rose. You don't paint its symbolism. Well you can, but not necessarily. You may paint it because it gives you pleasure: it may be just that. It is concentrated on in itself and if it has symbolic value it will yield itself up in the process of concentrating on its reality. . . . You start by looking at what happens in the play and an analysis of the action will tend to show you what the play means. But for an actor to work on the symbolic value of what he's doing is an absolute waste of time. He must always work on the specific and that's always been true in acting. It's as true of Stanislavsky as it is of Brecht. They are not at all at variance on this. They are both absolutely concerned with specifics: the psychological *specific*, the sociological *specific*. What time of day it is; what the weather is like; where you've come from; where you're going; what you're doing. All those things are specifics and if you come on playing a symbol it's hopeless. Symbolism only produces bad acting. You can't come on thinking, 'I am a symbol.' You see actors doing it but they're always terrible actors . . . what you get is a kind of Victorian style. You can make symbols but it's not to say the acting process is concerned with making symbols. Anything can be a symbol of anything; like money is a symbol of wealth. Every action is capable of symbolic interpretation, however practical and ordinary, and the theatre deals in that a lot: one action will stand for another. But you have to concentrate on the action itself for the symbol to work. If you work knowing what the symbol is then the action becomes blurred. I really believe that very strongly. I see its 'implications' if you like, in the work of Dorothy and its danger in the work of a lot of theatre practitioners. They work too directly towards the symbol. I don't think any good directors do that. I don't think Peter Brook works like that although he works in a very free way. I don't think he allows the interpretation to become part of the work. The interpretation's what people do afterwards: it's what the critics, the academicians do, afterwards. After you've made the thing, they tell you what it means. But in the making of it you shouldn't know.

KR: You shouldn't know what it means?

WG: You shouldn't know what its symbolic meaning is.

KR: And you don't know what it means?

WG: Well, when you're working on a text, sometimes the writer's symbols are clear. But it doesn't help the actor any, which is what I'm talking about – how the actor's creative mind functions. What I'm not going to do is ask him to be a symbol. I take it that he is a human being and that he's playing a human being. That's the process.

KR: So you're saying that, in thinking about the actors' creative energies, the director ought to have, or normally has, a general understanding of what the play is aiming to say but that you'd not want to encumber the actor with all the symbolic import of the piece because, if they become self-conscious about that, it would obstruct their working process.

WG: Yes. Absolutely.

KR: But as a director you're in a different position?

WG: Yes. As a director you're aware of the text on all kinds of levels including the symbolic. It's not the same thing as the actors' process of performing it on the stage or rehearsing it.

KR: You were saying that you see no reason why actors shouldn't think. Why shouldn't they be party to all of your thinking? Why shouldn't you encourage them to think about the over-all import of the play or the specific symbolism, where you recognize it, of the characters they're playing?

WG: Well they can. But it's dangerous if they think that it should be part of their *work* to use it. They're working on a much more realistic basis than that. Symbolism may lead them to sloppy work.

KR: Is that true of all actors?

WG: All actors who perform in plays. The work of groups like Cantor's Polish group where they are mainly artists – I mean painters, sculptors, working in a very plastic medium – is something different. But they deal through the plastic, they don't deal through the symbols. The director deals through the symbols. They deal as artists do, with images and images are quite different. Images are images and, whatever they may mean, artists don't worry too much about them, they like them for their own sake. I think that's true of a lot of creations.

WG: You began by saying that for the actors, the director stands for the audience. Is that always true of your work?

KR: It's true of all directors. All directors are the audience. They constantly simulate the audience. It's one of the main reasons for having a director. They need to constantly help the actors know if they are making it clear; are they exciting or amusing; are they comunicating?

KR: You obviously see the director having a number of other roles apart from this.

WG: Oh sure. But it's the one that's most important. It's the one they most need really.

KR: What is your main role for the actors apart from being a vicarious audience?

WG: There are many different things. The director is not only a teacher but a conductor and you know how musicians say, 'That director's no good, he talks too much'. I talk too much. I felt that Dorothy in her work with the actors talked too much. It blocks the actors' energy. When I let the audience talk too much it had the same effect. It drained the actors' energy and took up their time. That's why I eventually made a stong decision to concentrate on what the *actors* could do. One has to produce energy. I don't mean just more energy but more precise energy. You can measure the success of the work by how long the actors are working on the stage. At the best of course you record what they do, like a seismograph. You actually observe what it is that they have done in the scene so that you can play it back to them and analyse it as it goes along. That's apart from actually telling them where to stand and where to sit down, which you spend some time doing, or explaining the text to them. At its best, when you have actors who are very skilled, you just sit and watch them a lot of the time. You let them do an extended period of work and then stop and make suggestions. When you work out the details of anything physical or specific, you get up and move around with them; work out things *with* them; talk *to* them. Of course some directors work very closely with the actors on psychological viewpoints and they go very close and they whisper to the actors about their inner lives. But I've never done that. I don't really approve of that.

KR: Why don't you approve of it?

WG: Because it's not objective. You're not really in an outside position.
It's very important for a director to represent, as it were, some
kind of objective viewpoint from outside rather than the inner
workings of the psyche.

3. Theatre Form in Drama Teaching

Gavin Bolton

When I talk about my work in schools I call it drama. What I mean by the word has altered for me over the years. By drama do I still mean *not* theatre? Sometimes I insist on the term drama in education, for I am conscious that undergraduates in University Drama Departments refer to dramatic literature as drama, and I know that in schools I am not so much concerned with the *study* of drama as the *experience* of it.

The content of drama lessons, to use educational jargon, is interdisciplinary, for experience cuts across the subject disciplines. Through this experience, five-year-olds, fifteen-year-olds, twenty-five-year-olds and sixty-five-year-olds may have their understanding of themselves in relation to the world they live in reinforced, clarified or modified and secondly they may gain skills in social interaction which include the ability to communicate their understanding and feelings.

But does this experiencing of drama imply *not* experiencing theatre? The answer is NO and YES. I put NO first for only if we accept a distinction between the two which can never be ignored can we usefully pursue the common ground.

It is not easy to find the words to describe the experiencing of drama. The quality is perhaps best suggested by saying the process is a mixture of 'it is happening to me now; and I am making it happen now'. There are at least three features here, (1) a spontaneity (2) a 'nowness' that is tied to the future and, most importantly, (3) ME in the experience: 'It is happening to ME; *I* am making it happen. I am climbing Everest; I am being imprisoned; I am attending an enquiry about Windscale; I am to be brought out of hospital today; I am hiding from the Roundheads.'

In another sense, of course, it is not happening at all. It is a piece of fiction. The potential for learning lies in this very ambivalence that it is happening and yet not happening. So it is a metaphorical experience which still retains the spontaneity, the now-ness and the me-ness of an actual experience. It is because it retains such a close resemblance to living that teachers can harness this 'dramatic playing' to help children find and reflect upon all kinds of meanings that may not be available to them in their daily living.

Now if we move into theatre, the actors are in a very different order of experiencing, a difference that is crucial. The degree to which the actors can say 'it is happening to me now; and I am making it happen' is significantly reduced or overshadowed by an orientation towards interpretation, repeatability, projection and sharing with an audience. The reinforcement or clarification or modification not to mention the entertainment must ultimately be enjoyed by the audience.

I watched a child recently hiding from the Roundheads by getting behind the school piano. He was *actually* hiding, not really knowing whether or not he would be discovered. Deep in belief, he held his knuckles tight to his mouth. In theatre the actor may or may not use that gesture, but it is the audience who must, at least emotionally, hold their knuckles tight to their mouths. It seems to me that the art of acting is the drawing out of both an emotional response and, more important, a reflective response in an audience. For the child in drama the skill lies in behaving with integrity and spontaneity in a fictitious situation, not acting in the sense just described, but *being*.

But such dramatic playing can be superficial. Unless the living through is experienced with a sharpened consciousness, its value will be, at best, cathartic. It is the teacher's responsibility to help the children find significance in their work. And this is where, paradoxically, we find a common ground between drama and theatre, for the teacher uses the very elements of theatre that are normally the tools of the playwright. As the playwright focuses the meaning for the audience, so the teacher helps to focus meaning for the children; as the playwright builds tension for the audience; the teacher builds tension for the children; as the playwrights and director and actors highlight meaning for the audience by the use of contrast in sound, light and movement, so does the teacher – for the children; as the playwright chooses with great care the symbolic actions and objects that will operate at many levels of meaning for the audience, so will the teacher help the children find symbols in their work. The mode of the children's experience must continue as 'I am making it happen; it is happening to me'. I claim that when the teacher 'folds into' this mode a structure that would be valid for the playwright, then there is a greater chance of learning taking place.

To the question what have drama and theatre in common, my answer is that whereas there is no useful comparison between what the child does and what the actor is required to do, the two forms share the same basic structures.

THE TEACHER'S FUNCTION

The principal function of a drama teacher, then, is to use theatrical form in order to enhance the meaning of the participants' experience: by using the theatrical elements of tension, focus, contrast and symbolization, actions and objects in the drama become significant. I have suggested that this theatrical structuring is combined with the spontaneous existential mode of the participants. A useful parallel for comparison can be found in formal games. Such games as football, Monopoly, and tick'n hit are good examples of participants *experiencing* within a highly structured framework.

Both games and drama require commitment. Making a start with a game seems to be relatively easy, although one can imagine a group of adolescents, unquestionably committed to football, feeling rather unsure of tennis, and although intensely and secretly intrigued, nevertheless distrustful of the party game of 'consequences'.'

Whether it be a game or a drama, to start requires commitment; and drama is further complicated by requiring emotional engagement with the subject-matter. Another function of the drama teacher, therefore, is to work for commitment to drama and, more importantly, delicately to adjust the quality, degree and intensity of emotional engagement the topic arouses, so that the participants may with integrity, spontaneity and a sharpened consciousness enter the fictitious context. If some of the class are not interested in the topic, he may have to 'capture' their interest; if they are interested but inhibited by it, he may have to work to make it safe; if they are over-excited, he may have to contain their excitement.

Thus another purpose to teacher-structuring is emerging. Often a teacher cannot use theatrical form to enhance meaning, that is to bring about some change in the participants' understanding of a topic, until steps are taken to modify the emotional loading that topic carries for a particular class. He often finds himself structuring the dramatic activity in order to change the 'emotional temperature' as it were. The three lessons at the Riverside Studios are good examples of a teacher working towards this end.

Before I describe them I would like to share with you the 'luggage' I take with me into a classroom.

A PERFECT DRAMA LESSON

I suppose every drama teacher has at the back of his mind some notion of a model educational drama experience. It is unlikely to be of the kind that I was once taught – if you have exercised all five senses you have had a good lesson! It may not have any particular shape or content or steps. It may be just a vague sense of direction, or a series of hunches about inner experiences. However unfettered with plans a teacher may be, he must walk into the classroom with some kind of expectations.

In *my* dreams the perfect school drama experience round the corner will look something like this:

Expectations of Class
1. They know that drama is for understanding.
2. They know it requires patient, reflective, hard work both in and out of the activity.
3. They know it only works if they contribute with an openness and critical awareness.
4. They know it is an art form in *process* not product.

Trust
1. They trust the situation; trust the teacher; trust each other; trust drama – indeed they are committed to it.

Selection
1. They agree (this perfect class are bound to I suppose!) on a topic that is important to them.

2. Through discussion it emerges in what way it is important. They are neither over- nor under-stimulated by the subject-matter.

The Drama

1. They or their teacher select (this is the playwright's function) a focus for starting the action, an action that carries some kind of tension, an action (and any properties used) that is susceptible or potentially susceptible to symbolic meanings.

2. They work with commitment in five directions: (i) they work in anticipation that something is going to be learnt from the situation; (ii) they work for credibility; (iii) they find a feeling quality that is appropriate to the fictitious context; (iv) they work towards form; (v) they take risks so they can experience.

The Teaching

1. Teacher introduces some theatre strategy to help extend, deepen, change the perspective or simply make explicit their understanding of the chosen theme.

2. If selected with care (and in this model lesson everything is done with care!) the strategy meets other important objectives such as language development, increase in social responsibility etc.

3. The theatrical form is such that actions and objects resonate meanings of both personal and group significance.

The Outcome

1. The satisfaction they found in the experience leads them to want to reflect upon it in a way that is productive.

2. It becomes a significant future reference point for them in their own lives.

It would be nice, just once, to experience this perfect model in practice just to find out whether it really is — perfect, that is!

What gives it unifying direction is the assumption that the main target of the drama work is some change in understanding. This does not imply that if you don't get there, you have failed. It is rather like intending to go on a journey. You may find out that you are not ready to reach the destination you have in mind, but you looked at maps and packed *as if* you were going to get there. The map work and the packing turn out to be worthwhile experiences in themselves *because they were carried out purposefully*.

The point that I am making is that the assumption behind all drama must be that it will lead to some change of understanding – of oneself in relation to the world one lives in, an assumption that a playwright might not unreasonably have about the effect of his play on an audience. It is this assumption that gives any use of drama its dynamic: whatever limitations there may be, whatever immediate problems one finds oneself dealing with, whatever temporary goal one finds oneself pursuing, this over-all purpose characterizes all the variety of activities that can go under the name of a drama lesson. This is an assumption that is not always shared by the children themselves. Very often one meets children for whom drama has no over-all purpose, children who have had drama too sporadically for them to have grasped anything about it, or who have been implicitly taught that drama means 'fun', or 'getting rid of surplus energy', or 'learning acting tricks', or 'an escape from reality'. In other words, children too bring luggage to the classroom, a factor again well illustrated at the Riverside Studios. Let me now begin to describe as fully as is useful in terms of the above discussion, what happened during the three weekend sessions.

THREE LESSONS

The Riverside Studios teaching was a very happy experience for me – apart from the second of the three lessons which I handled ineptly. But the pleasure I derived did not stem from a destination reached in terms of changing those pupils' level of thinking and understanding, although I would claim that the potential for doing so, given a third and fourth lesson, was there. (I can hear some readers at this point either muttering 'The arrogance of the man!' or, as one commentator said during Sunday turkey luncheon – 'You have spent three long lessons[1] achieving nothing!')

'Change in understanding' implies an affective/cognitive shift in the topic. This class of lower band twelve-year-olds chose: 'Violence in schools'. As it turned out, the intellectual learning, although providing the dynamic, was peripheral to the real learning that appeared to be going on. It seemed to me that for most of the three lessons we were finding an appropriate level of emotion and, in this respect I believe important things were happening. But first let me give you the bare-bones, the *external* features of the lesson sequences.

Lesson One

1. The class are invited to choose a topic. The most popular two topics from the class's four suggestions were 'Violence' and 'School'. They put the two together so that the topic for the drama became 'Violence in School'.
2. A 'school staff-meeting' is held with me in role as headmaster, to discuss the outrageous behaviour of a particular class – a fifth year as it turned out.
3. Out of role, in small groups, they discuss the kind of outrageous behaviour they want it to be and select, 'throwing food about in the dining-room'.
4. A further staff-meeting to discuss punishment to fit the crime.
5. Role-play in pairs – as adolescents reporting to each other 'what happened in the school dining-room today!'

Lesson Two

1. On a long roll of paper, they draw or describe all the public places like clubs and X film cinemas that are open to sixteen-year-olds, but not to twelve-year-olds.
2. I then role-play a journalist trying to get some gossip for my paper from the 'notorious' adolescents about the dining-room incident.
3. Out of role, we select the class 'ring-leaders' and look at their attitude to school.
4. In role, just using two or three children at a time, with the rest of the class watching, we explore attitudes of their parents to school.
5. They all move into small groups of 'ring-leader' families to rehearse the moment when the parents first hear about the 'incident'.

Lesson Three

1. They 'show', in each family how each ring-leader is received when he gets home from school (the parents just having heard the school's version first).
2. They become the troublesome fifth year class, after having indicated to me what kind of class teacher (in role) they want me to play.

3. They become staff again – except for the ring-leaders – holding a staff meeting to make final decisions about punishment, now that they are better informed of the various attitudes to the incident.

I now propose, using the above three outlines as reference points, to discuss teacher structuring in terms of commitment and emotional adjustment.

TRUST

From the very start the children at Riverside found themselves in a situation they could not trust, not simply because of the place and the milling throng of adults, but because of the expectations of drama that they brought with them. Apart from the covert hints during the first lesson, their assumptions about drama were made clear to me in the lunch break. They made but three comments about the experience so far:

> 'We were told we would play games.'
> 'When are we going to get into our groups to act something for them (the audience)?'
> 'We don't have to carry on with the same thing next lesson do we – we don't at school?'

Already the first section of my model lesson is scrubbed! So here we have a class and teacher with two different sets of luggage as it were. Everything he does says 'process'; everything they do says 'product'. They say short-term; he says long-term. He says 'learning'; they say 'games'. Could anything be more threatening to a group of twelve-year-olds especially in physical surroundings with banked rows of 'short stay' spectators, a context clearly signalling to the children that product, games and short term would be more appropriate.

Now I know that given these special circumstances, it is very tempting to reduce the feeling of threat by letting them play games etc. This would seem the right step to many teachers and, possibly, to theatre people. But I know with my whole rational and irrational self that that is exactly what I must *not* do. The most important thing I have to teach is that an art form is for understanding. So from the outset, I am going to make a painful situation more painful by pulling in the opposite direction from the one in which they want to go. But of course I will do all I can as a person to build trust in *other* ways: for example, to signal to them that I understand what they are going through and protect them during the journey as much as possible.

Once this dynamic of a purposeful destination is established, however, I can use their luggage, often luggage they did not know they had brought with them. For instance, on this particular occasion, as you can see from above, they were entirely responsible for the choice of topic; in choosing violent behaviour, they were free to indicate what they wanted that behaviour to be; towards the end of the second lesson they had the chance they seemed to want to rehearse in small groups.

But these freedoms were heavily countered by restrictions imposed by me: my insistence that most of the time we worked as a whole group; the slowness of pace; a good deal of sitting and talking. These represent the external features of a slow, thoughtful process that is nearly always necessary if pulling in the opposite direction (I say nearly always — sometimes sudden shock tactics switch the direction at one stroke!). There are risks of course. Teaching is about weighing up risks. You may bore them to death, a natural reaction from a class who feel that they ought to be 'getting on'. Signs of this emerged strongly in the second lesson. It is when they begin to see glimmers of compensation that they begin to trust the teacher and the situation: their hearts may sink when they find themselves gathered round a black-board but may lift again when it is *their* thinking that goes up on the board. And what they learn eventually of course, true of all creative work, is that the apparently endless troughs lead to richer peaks — as they discovered in the third lesson. But if they have been taught by 'Let's-get-up-and-go-for-drama-is-doing' teachers they will be unlikely to know this pain/joy of creativity.

One restriction I imposed is a significant one which leads us into a discussion of the central feature of the experience: emotional engagement with the subject-matter. The topic the class unanimously chose was a combination of 'violence' and 'classroom'. Hearing this decision some members of the audience of actors and teachers assumed that the proper thing to do would be for me to let the class dramatically have their 'violent' experience. This would give a useful reference point for extending their thinking and also be a means of letting them 'let off steam' in a controlled way. I think they assumed that because

I did not let this happen, I was protecting myself by dodging the experience.

Now this point of view, well articulated after the lesson was over and subsequently repeated by my Sunday lunch critic, is opposite to my own and is worth examining in some detail, in the next section.

PROTECTING

Whether you are a professional actor in an improvisation or a child in symbolic play the integrity of the experience will depend upon the quality of feeling you bring to the activity. The feeling must be appropriate to the context. If the child or actor, for example, bursts into a fit of giggles or passes some witticism as he is being chased by a killer shark, unless the pre-decided form is comedy, we could reasonably agree that feeling and context were incompatible. Getting into the action of drama is an approximating process of finding a quality of feeling that matches one's understanding of the theme and context. It is often very difficult in fact for children, however well-intentioned and however genuine their interest in the topic, to evoke appropriate feeling quality. Grief and ecstasy, for example, cannot be easily tapped. Much depends of course on the mood the pupils are in before the drama starts. If they are particularly happy and excited about something, it might be comparatively easy to transfer that mood to a drama about ecstasy. Equally, a child with a recent bereavement, will perhaps only too readily call upon a feeling of grief.

Thus the emotional starting point for dramatic action is initially dependent upon where a class is emotionally, at the *actual* level. It seems to me that there are two broad bands of emotion – the introverting and the extroverting, i.e. closing and opening, or momentum-reducing and action-impelling. For instance, compare shyness and boldness, or quiet amusement and ecstasy, or riveted with fear and fleeing in fear, or (more relevant here) feeling threatened and being threatening. If a group of children or adults choose a topic that happens immediately to demand an expression of feeling that is poles apart from their actual feelings then the starting point for the fiction must somehow legitimately cater for their actual feelings: an *oblique* way into the theme must be found. It is no use expecting a class of sullen, reluctant fourteen-year-olds to act out a cheerful birthday party ('Come on now, how would you feel?', one might find oneself asking hopefully!). Nor would you, faced with an eager, fun-seeking class of twelve-year-olds saying, 'Let's do a play where we get frightened by ghosts' start the drama with the ghosts' arrival!

Now a 'violence in school' theme requires a release of aggressive, hostile or angry feelings or some extrovert feeling of that order, in marked contrast to what was actually felt by that Riverside Studio class of children, who were clearly threatened and wracked with self-consciousness. One quite popular way round this problem is to turn to 'acting'. In many schools we have trained children to 'switch on' imitative emotional display, so that they give a *demonstration* of anger and hostility in a way that has little to do with real feeling. We sometimes mistakenly think that this is what a professional actor does. Our theatre schools know only too well the effort that some of their students have to put into *unlearning* these glib techniques. Unfortunately many children, given a taste for superficiality, resist working at finding an appropriate feeling quality. At Riverside it was my responsibility to show the class an alternative way of working.

So the only way it seems to me is to 'protect' them into a context that does not expose, a context that naturally permits them to indulge an 'introverting' emotion while gradually opening up the topic. It is also flexible enough to allow, as some of the class break from their self-consciousness, a change in feeling quality. Thus it was we became a staff meeting with me as head-master (again they must be allowed to *lean* – another example of my giving support after having threatened). As they gained in confidence some of them began the next key move – working for credibility; picking up the rules of the game and beginning to use them creatively.

NEGOTIATING MEANING

This phrase, coined by the Schools Council Secondary Drama Project[2], is a useful way of describing the delicate, uncovering process that follows. The 'staff-room' structure for the 'protecting' purpose as discussed above, also fulfils this vitally important function of negotiating meaning.

The class has chosen violence in schools. This could mean *anything* depending so much on their backgrounds, attitudes to school and to violence, etc. As teacher I need to find out what *they* mean or I cannot do anything about extending that meaning. So often as a teacher I find myself with even the best of intentions working at what *I* mean by violence or some such topic. Now by initially placing the children in a school situation, but as a staff not as pupils, I am giving them a chance at more than one remove, to indicate what the 'kicks' are to be for them. For as staff they can let imaginations work in any direction that is most satisfying. Getting in touch with one's private desires and dreams and wishes is a thought process that can often only be made public in a form that is indirect, so that shifting to an off-centre activity is a fairly typical piece of structuring for emotionally charged topics. It was not insignificant that very early in the 'staff meeting' when asked by me what form in school was creating the most trouble, they seized the chance to distance it further by saying 'a fifth year'.[3]

My expectation of what they would offer when given the chance to describe the violence of this fictitious fifth year verged, I suspect, on something sensational, but what we actually got was:

'Being caught climbing through a window'.
'Taking your trousers down in front of the girls in the classroom'.
'Mixing mud into the food in the dining room'.
'Throwing food at the cooks'.

They chose the last two. So they are not really after *violence* as such but some form of *school illegality*. It was interesting that some of the fantasy imagery that later arose from one or two of the children in the 'ring-leader's homes' came nearer to a concept of violence and the macabre. We proceeded from there to look at the reported 'terrible incident in the dining room' from the point of view of teachers, parents and ring-leaders – all *after* the event. I know that they must not be trapped into experiencing that fifth year class of anti-social pupils until they are really ready for it. But there is something about this particular topic that is in itself unique and consequently creates a set of special emotional circumstances that are both an opportunity and a problem for all the participants – including teacher!

Before we move into this, however, there is an important point that I want to take up to do with what I understand by *acting* in drama as a process. One of the adult spectators (I do not know whether it was an actor or a teacher — it would have been interesting to find out) commented dismissively during the lesson to a neighbour: 'How can he expect twelve-year-olds to act sixteen-year-olds?' Now to ask this question shows in my view a total misunderstanding of the educational function. Drama provides an opportunity for the participant to find out about himself in any context. The valuable metaphorical experience lies in a juxtaposition between the child and the role he has selected. As I said above 'It is happening to *me* now'. It is not that he has *become* someone else nor is it that if he is role-playing a sixteen-year-old there is some standard recognizable performance that has to be reached. The only objective criteria that must be met are those that he needs to make his role credible to himself and to his classmates. This point is made even more effectively where, as it turned out in this case, the children were not interested in sixteen-year-olds as such but only as a mask behind which they could indulge their fantasies. The role is merely a reference point for something more important.

CONTAINING AND HARNESSING EMOTION

The peculiarity of the topic they happen to have chosen — illegal behaviour in school — is that its personal and group reference points are equally strong, in that the topic not only offers personal excitement but is also very near to their actual situation. They are a school class role-playing a school class — a context that is ripe for both individual and group fantasy trips. This could be emotional dynamite! Robert Witkin in his book *Intelligence of Feeling* has written about this kind of situation and its dangers: 'Sometimes teachers do operate with dramatic situations that threaten to permeate the barrier between the simulated network (the relationships and the dramatic situation) and the real network (relationships among pupils and between teachers and pupils)[4]. He then goes on to describe a particularly unhealthy instance of a third year secondary group enacting head teacher/pupil roles as a way of dealing with a set of *real* problems with their own head teacher — a direct use of dramatic role play that, if it must be used, requires more expert handling than most teachers are trained for.

But the Riverside instance, although different in kind from Witkin's example, is not without its hazards.

These three lessons presented an extraordinary emotional sequence – for once the class were protected and led from their own introverting emotion, with this particular context group extroversion could be released like a thunder storm!

What are the possible safeguards[5] in such a situation? One of them is that the role play is nominally at one remove – they are sixteen-year-olds; it is the formidable, fictitious 5Q that is the centre of concern. Indeed during the first lesson when they labelled the class 5D – a real class in their own school – I insisted that we were in some other school – and with a class with an unfamiliar title. Another safeguard lies in the tightness of teacher structuring. The third lesson was planned in three clearly defined phases which were explained to the class at the beginning of the lesson: 1. small group 'showing' of how different sets of parents received their 5Q child after the event had been reported; 2. a 5Q classroom episode; 3. a staff meeting. The third safe-guard is teacher's planning for affective/cognitive change. I intended to use the double experience of their being the 'terrible 5Q' with me as their 'teacher', followed by a final staff meeting in which they, now as staff, would be required to counter their own arguments expressed earlier in their role as 5Q. That the potential for such learning is there and that teacher is constantly looking for an opportunity to promote it, is a crucial feature of the structuring. But the class denied themselves this opportunity by hardening their position as a badly behaved class into a class with power over their 5Q teacher!

Now I know this alarmed many of the spectators, but in fact as long as they are required to work symbolically within the theatre form, far from being dangerous, it requires the most disciplined behaviour. In other words it becomes a fourth safeguard. *Dramatically* the experience of being 5Q gives them enormous freedom (I was told afterwards by one of the spectators, one of their own teachers, that it was the quietest girls in the class who 'threatened me with a knife' during the scene), but *psychologically* that freedom is taken away, for they are bound by the rules of working symbolically[6]: they are *released into self discipline*. During that classroom scene the teacher's bag was stolen, the blackboard overturned and he was physically threatened, all of which, I am sure, sounds alarming, but every action was a *symbol* of power, not a raw expression of power. The question undoubtedly arises and indeed was hurriedly discussed after the lesson whether such an experience gives children a taste for power. Some people felt these children might now return to their school with the intention of challenging authority. I have not done any follow-up on this, but I would be very surprised if this was so. I have not developed a rationale to support it, but my hunch is that this kind of drama experience has the opposite effect and is really no more alarming that a four-year-old saying to his mother: 'I'll be your mummy and you be my child' and then sets out to symbolize all sorts of extreme 'mummy behaviours'. The danger comes of course when the children are not working within an art form at all, as in the instance described by Robert Witkin, when their actions are no longer symbolic.

Another safeguard in this kind of fantasy trip is that teacher continues to hold firmly on the reins in two directions. Having noted the implied consensus of agreement by the class on the degree to which objective reality must be met in order for their fantasy context to have credibility, the teacher will then insist that they either keep to that degree or increase it: he will not tolerate a further slide away from objectivity. Connected with this is that whatever reality is found within the fiction it will have its own logic, its own rules: again it is a teacher's responsibility to insist that the class keep to that logic. Some-times an over-excited or particularly egocentric child will break the implied rules and distort the fantasy beyond the class's intentions, again challenging credibility. The teacher must step in on these occasions – as indeed I had to during the staffroom scene.

Another safeguard is that I have no qualms whatsoever at stopping the progress of the drama. Indeed I establish with most classes that I shall often hold up the drama for us to examine what we are creating. I often use the device that 'When I move to this chair we are no longer in role'. So I constantly put a brake on the dramatic flow, not to hold some intellectual discussion, but to check on the integrity of the experience.

It was a pleasurable experience for me to work with that class as we searched together for a viable dramatic form. By lesson three they were struggling as a group to discipline their release of energy – and they succeeded – just! One commentator had remarked, 'All that surplus energy – why doesn't he let them play games?' I hope he would share with me the satisfaction of this degree of energy purposefully and dramatically harnessed: I don't want to get rid of it; I want to use it – but it takes time. I saw this as a satisfying, important step forward that the class and I had taken together. We smiled at each other in our farewells – a sharing of a new understanding that was full of promise should we meet and do drama again.

And then, over my plate piled with turkey: 'These children are at the same level of thinking they were at when you started and you have had far longer than most teachers ever get.' I returned my plate (still piled with turkey!) and pondered. Here was someone using the very criteria I use myself: 'Has the drama broken these children's stereotyped thinking?' The answer must be that my critic is unreservedly right. Then why was I so pleased with myself? What do I think they had learned?

The answer lies in the headings of this chapter: trust; protection; negotiation of meaning; and containing. I claim that each of these is a worthwhile experience for me and the class to share. But more than that I would be satisfied if I could guarantee that they have learned three vitally important things:

1. a new sensing of dramatic form and a glimmer of what works in the dramatic process
2. at least a tentative grasp that drama is for understanding – this is its *purpose*
3. that this understanding is reached through finding an integrity of feeling.

I would not expect that the children themselves could articulate these points. If indeed I have planted these seeds then that class and I are ready to move forward with leaps and bounds. I may have achieved in three lessons (three *long consecutive* lessons) what it takes teachers with their one hour a week six months to achieve – and what those confined to thirty-five minutes periods have little chance of achieving.

Conclusion

In this chapter I have attempted to discuss two teacher functions that are critical to the drama teacher's work. The peculiarity of the choice of topic by the Riverside children, their own expectations of what drama is and the circumstances in which they found themselves, stressed the first of these functions: working for commitment, for an experimental as opposed to an 'acting' mode of behaviour and towards stimulating or tempering emotional engagement with the theme. The second function is to move in the direction of change of understanding. The structures that are available to a teacher in carrying out both functions are often the structures employed by the playwright. A drama teacher is consistently working in theatre form.

Heathcotewold disagree?

4. From the Universal to the Particular

Nicholas Wright

One of the aims of the Riverside Conference was to suggest ways in which the working methods of drama teachers and theatre artists might be usefully compared. The demonstrations led by Dorothy Heathcote, Gavin Bolton and William Gaskill were intended to be seen not independently but in relation to each other, the discussions sandwiched between them being concentrated on ways in which their techniques appeared to differ, overlap or match. On the whole, finding similarities was regarded as a 'good thing'. Similar techniques would suggest a common aim; common aims would make possible a readier exchange between drama teachers and theatre artists and perhaps even mellow the edginess which often exists between them.

Certain difficulties appeared, not that they were always recognized. Where differences in approach yawned between Dorothy Heathcote and William Gaskill, for example, they tended to be viewed hopefully as transient hiccups in a progressive process of drawing together. To suggest, in this context, that similarities between working methods of drama teachers and theatre artists may be superficial or coincidental, serving only to mask essential differences, may seem divisive, unconstructive, even Scrooge-like. But this is the case.

Features in common don't prove a common aim. Working methods imported from one activity to the other may come to serve a different function altogether, much as the Bible stops being a book of wisdom when it is used to prop up the piano.

The relationship between theatre and drama teaching is peculiar and interesting. After all, children taught painting produce paintings; music classes produce music. But although it may be part of the work of a drama class to produce plays, this is neither a necessity nor the usual objective. Drama, as part of a school curriculum, need not produce anything to be watched. Nor is class-room drama the equivalent of practising scales on the violin or drawing sketches for future paintings. It is an activity *sui generis*.

In the following reflections on drama and theatre I want to ignore all apparent resemblances between working methods. There is after all a problem in knowing to which theatre worker the drama teacher is to be compared. The playwright? The director? The actor? I want instead to compare drama and theatre, as social practices, in terms of their social functions and argue that:

1. It is a function of theatre *as entertainment* to make moral and political statements.
2. These statements are always recognized as *relative* and *objective* because of certain limitations inherent in the nature of theatre *as an art form* which define the context in which these statements are being made.
3. By contrast the statements which are made in drama teaching – which are also moral and political – *appear absolute* and *universal* because they are *not* placed in context.

I want to describe what these limitations on theatre are and then look critically at this aspect of drama teaching by considering the nature of the context in which it does take place.

There is an important proviso to all of this. In the interests of clarity and brevity I will be using the word 'theatre' without qualification. I am referring, however, specifically and perhaps only to theatre in the industrialized West.

THE ARTIST: A PROBLEM OF DEFINITION

Theatre is characterized by (1) the number of people who (2) share responsibility for producing (3) the work of art. While few plays have casts the size of a symphony orchestra, no orchestral player has such scope for personal interpretation as an actor, director, designer or playwright. To say that a theatrical performance is the responsibility of a group, however, is not to say that its members share the same interests. Each member of a theatre company has some power to control the final product, but this power varies in degree from member to member. To exactly this degree the interests of individuals will jar or conflict. The team behind a performance, far from being the headmaster's dream of a group united by a single aim, may be a temporary alliance between warring factions and individuals, one close to the heart of creation, another comparatively alienated.

A theatre artist's relation to the work of art he helps to produce, and the extent of his responsibility for it, is ultimately determined by his relations of employment. The two can never be separated. Star actors get, not only a higher salary and a percentage of the takings, but more influence over the piece as a whole than the other actors. The commercial manager stands to make or lose most and is final arbiter, etc., etc. These are crude examples of a process which affects everyone who works on a play.

In Britain today, the theatre artist's work-relations vary a great deal according to the company he works for. Theatre mirrors whatever society produces it. In feudal society, actors fed in the kitchen, if they were lucky. The rise of the private entrepreneur was followed by the appearance of the actor-manager, employer of his fellows, knighted/damed and buried in Westminster Abbey. When such pirates went out of fashion, the monolithic structure of the multi-national corporation, together with its anxiously pluralist façade, was parodied in National Theatres, and so on. This is natural: whatever is happening in society is the bricks and mortar of theatre. Theatre's quick response to social contradictions has resulted today in an appropriately shattered reflection of a fragmented and mixed society. In most professions members share the same relations of employment as each other on the same level of eminence. Theatre presents a Breughelesque landscape in which the palace nudges the pigsty and the gamekeeper rubs shoulders with the poacher.

John Ashford once usefully noted five separate groups within what is unhelpfully called Fringe Theatre:

1. Companies presenting new plays by new authors, e.g. The Bush or The Theatre Upstairs.
2. Companies experimenting with form rather than with content, e.g. Triple Action Theatre or (then) Freehold.
3. Visual Theatre/Happenings, e.g. The People Show, Welfare State.
4. Community Theatre Companies, e.g. The Natural Theatre.

5. 'Political' Companies, e.g. CAST, Red Ladder.

All form but a small subdivision of our subsidized theatre, which includes two giants – the National and the Royal Shakespeare Company – an ugly duckling – the Royal Court – and a host of regional theatres. If the cabin now seems crowded, the weightiest passenger has yet to struggle to its bunk: the commercial theatre, a massive employer and purveyor of goods.

In each of these areas, labour is divided in a different way. In so-called 'writers' theatre', the entire team consider they are serving the writer's interests. In a community theatre company this is unlikely to be the case: the writer may become a kind of stenographer providing dramatic images rather than typed letters. However, in such a company the actors may feel closer to their work than in any other employ, willingly loading the van in the knowledge that they're their own bosses and that no-one is benefitting from their extra labours other than their audiences and themselves.

When comparing theatre and drama, it is important to note these variations of artistic responsibility. Common areas exist across the board between drama teachers in a way they don't between theatre workers. They all teach; they all belong to the professional classes; nearly all work in institutions. Methods vary, but the teachers share the same function. Similarly, although the particular personal relationships between teachers and children may vary, the material relationship does not. We will search the theatre in vain for a stratum of workers whose role is so clearly defined and whose responsibility for the work is so concrete.

In order to make comparison possible, I propose to invent a figure: *the artist*. He is unlikely to be a single man or woman; he may be two or three, and is more likely to be two or three dozen. The artist is not exclusively the playwright, whose intentions are modified by the actors; nor the actors, who interpret the play under some degree of control by the director. Nor have the collective efforts of the 'artistic' members of the ensemble much autonomy from the person or institution responsible for the time, place and conditions of performance. These factors are usually determined by different, economic considerations, rather than by those we traditionally call 'artistic'. But we are bound for the present purpose to call them artistic, if only to recognize their potent ability to transform the meaning of the play.

When I speak of the artist, I refer to a bundle of varying responsibilities for the *gesture* of the play; responsibilities exercised in one case by writing, in others by directing and performing, or by the use of money. In the commercial theatre, for example, the impresario largely controls both the choice of play and the nature of its presentation. His employees understand that the point of the exercise is to make money and recognize him as the expert on the subject. Insofar as the impresario is responsible for the gesture of the play, he is the artist.

THE GESTURE

The *gesture* of the play is the most lasting impression the audience receives. It may be encapsulated in speech, physical gesture and tableau at some point of the evening, or, as in the epic theatre of Brecht, by a succession of such fleeting moments throughout the play. It may be coalesced in Ibsen's 'scene of obligation' – an inevitable passage of confrontation where the issues of the play collide. It may be overt and local: 'Gays Come Out.' It may, in the English manner, ripple through the play, disguised as the terms of reference against which the play acquires a sense of humour. For example, the comedy of Tom Stoppard's seemingly intricate play *Travesties* rests on the audience inferring that Tristan Tzara, James Joyce, Lenin and an obscure British diplomat were equally boobies and that we already know as much about them as we need.

The gesture of a play is its moral centre, which is to say it is political. Theatre exists within society. Its statements are invariably interpreted by the audience as being about society. To the extent that the audience has a political life of its own, it will have a political response to the play. However, this is not at all the same thing as saying that the play will necessarily make the slightest difference to the audience's future behaviour or change its mind in any way. Put differently, theatre is a *feature* of society's political and social life; but it remains to be seen whether it can in turn affect that life, or, if so, how. This troubles companies of the left (so-called 'political' companies) far more than it does managers and impresarios – the artists of the commercial sector – though their work is equally of a political nature.

It would be very naive to imagine that commercial managers

consciously put together a bourgeois package every time in order to attract the traditionally bourgeois theatre-going audience. The fact is that commercial impresarios put on the plays they do because they like them, and the audiences come, when they do, because they like them too. (When this audience, now dwindling, approaches extinction, managers will probably discover the aesthetic virtues of some other kind of theatre altogether. Punk? Ethnic minorities? We shall see.) Ideology is not *used* as a tool for digging up profit. Rather, it encloses merchant and customer alike, as invisibly as a glass bowl to the goldfish inside.

Within is a brisk trade in striking political images. Poofs mince across the stage hand on hip. Argentina tries not to cry at the sad death of Eva Peron. South African blacks boogie in delight at the thought of yet another village wedding.

These examples (all on sale as I write) are extremely obvious ones. But each of the countless acts of invention and selection which add up to form the structure of the play produces a distinct resonance. Each word spoken reveals the speaker's social status. Each physical movement indicates the character's response to his social environment: impatient, wearily tolerant, cynical, content. It would be possible to progress towards decoding the meaning inherent in the layout of the furniture and the shape of the carpet. Do they suggest order or chaos? Permanence or transition? How is the audience encouraged to respond to the world the play presents? With approval? With mockery? With anger?

At the Royal Court Theatre I once had an interesting conversation with a commercial manager, with whom we were co-presenting a play, about the colour of the leading lady's Act II dress. He objected to the fact that it was all the same colour – i.e., not separates. (Red, I think.) When I asked him what was wrong with it he patiently explained: 'Too West Endy.' What he meant was: traditionally, in the West End, leading actresses have some discretion about what they wear. Very often they choose a costume in a single, striking colour in order to show up better against the set. (And of course the other actors.)

However, this production was taking place at the Royal Court, the home of serious (i.e. non-commercial) theatre. If it looked like an ordinary West End production, the reviews would suffer and the chances of a transfer to the West End, which is where the impresario would make his profit, would be jeopardized. The investment capital had to be concealed in order to be re-couped at a later date.

Left-wing theatre is described as political because its political statements are conscious and explicit. Necessarily so: they are in conflict with the dominant bourgeois ideology. Political statements in bourgeois theatre are usually unconscious, camouflaged as aesthetics, and unrecognised even by their own authors.

Are political statements made in the drama class? Certainly moral values are there to be inferred. The extent to which they are or aren't political is something I'll discuss later.

FORM AS CONTEXT

Before pressing on to a direct comparison between drama teaching and theatre it is necessary to look at the *form* in which the artist in the theatre makes statements. Form in the theatre is not, of course, accidental; it is characterized by a number of calculated limitations on the *extent* of the play. These limitations serve as terms of reference, within which conflicts and incongruities become, not a jumble of meaninglessly assorted thematic squabbles, but sharp contradictions *between* which the meaning of the play lies.

Plays are consciously limited (1) in time (2) in space and (3) in 'world-view'.

Time

Unlike, say, painting or literature, plays exist strongly in time. Rehearsals take place literally against time. They are dominated by a timespan which cannot be predicted, and which is the subject of endless conjecture: the time-span of the audience's interest. There appears, sometimes, to be an almost mechanical limit to the duration of a play[1]; within this limit, the use, the *deployment* of time is a constant rehearsal preoccupation. Is it too slow? Is the pace too unvaried? If rehearsals go badly, still more if previews are discouraging, the attention to time becomes obsessive. Passages of wit and charm, excellent in themselves, are ruthlessly scrapped where they close in on the pace of the narrative. The tempo is here stretched, there (more usually) accelerated, in order for the passage of time to be disguised.

of education, and the relations of production of education, are owned and controlled by the Department of Education, which is to say the State. The type of education which the state provides expresses its characteristic ideology.

It may be argued that theatre also expresses the dominant ideology. It often does. However, enforcement of attendance is the critical factor.

ON THE AUTONOMY OF SELF-EXPRESSION

It may seem paradoxical to associate drama with indoctrination when self-expression is reckoned to play a central role in its teaching methods; when classes are characterized by a lack of emphasis on conventional skills and where, in drama jargon, 'subjective experience is used as a tool for learning'.

This aspect of drama is worth a look. It's often claimed of a drama exercise that 'the kids worked it out themselves'. Here, apparently, a blow has been struck for democracy: the teacher has ducked the odium of an authoritarian role, and the children have found the means to self-expression.[4]

But nobody carries about a sort of reservoir of pure 'self' which can be 'expressed' at the turn of a tap. Moreover in a classroom, however open-minded the teacher may be, the relationship between teacher and students is clouded by features quite outside the teacher's control. There is a conspicuous disparity of age, status and dependency between the partners. And on the deepest level the context remains one of compulsory participation.

If we recognize the ideological nature of this context we can see the extent to which even the child's own subjective attitudes will be ideologically formed. This is not to say that children are *never* able to arrive at the truth by themselves. But it is to insist that their subjective experience cannot be viewed independently of its context; that it may be most misleading where it is most convincing or intense; and that it needs at all times to be measured against objective fact.

UNIVERSAL TRUTH

Along with other forms of self-expression, drama enjoys some freedom from the tyranny of fact and information which for many years seemed to dominate education. There's a consequent danger: the temptation of inventing pseudo-facts, statements generally of a moral nature, which, though mere matters of opinion, products of a particular ideological context, are presented as though they were of absolute and permanent value.

In fact, once opinion has shaken off any finicky attachment to *material* facts, the most dazzling leaps become possible. This can be clearly seen in Mrs Heathcote's discovery of an entirely new category of fact: the universal truth.

I quote, as an example of this, a statement by Josephine Miles, referred to by Dorothy Heathcote as 'basic to the way I work': 'Art gives shape to the valued materials of life, in order that they may be stressed, attended to and preserved.' The phrase is an evocative one; the image springs to mind of roll upon roll of valued material nestling on the top shelf of a family haber-dashers. What are these materials? By whom are they valued? Are they equally valued by everybody?

Where does this leave the plays of Joe Orton? They share one consistent theme: that the customer needs only to poke a finger at these valued materials – be they law, marriage, sexual morality, whatever – and they will crumble like the wrappings on a mummy.

Art is under *no* obligation to reinforce conventional values. It may, and on the other hand it may not. It may disrupt them with anarchy, or it may expose them to reason.

When Dorothy Heathcote read Brecht's poem 'The Playwright's Song', she brought the second of these two ap-proaches into the centre of the arena. Of all modern writers, Brecht has most consciously written plays to be used as tools of reason. No playwright has taken more care to define his terms. Each character's social status is precisely shown; the economic factors underlying the drama are explained; the intellectual framework within which the conflicts of the play are fought out is clearly displayed.

For this reason the poem, accompanied by Heathcote's com-mentary, provides a particularly useful contrast between truth (particular) and truth (universal).

Without the commentary the poem is clear. It describes the social conditions of life in a certain country at a certain time, and it does so from a Marxist point of view. Men's lives are traded like commodities; people who can't be bribed are brutally attacked; people's most basic functions – eating, making love – are tainted with greed and violence. It is the poet's job to expose these things.

In this context, people who 'step into each other's rooms' should be resisted by all available means, intending as they do (a) to entangle the inmates of the room in schemes, (b) to bludgeon them with truncheons or (c) give them cash for (the poem implies) no good end. This is why it's so surprising when Heathcote uses Brecht's phrase to describe her own work. Fortunately it is clear she and Brecht mean quite different things by it.

The society which Brecht condemns is no longer something to be fought, but something to be understood, and, by implication, accommodated. To 'step into each others' rooms' describes an imaginative leap into the feelings and perceptions of others. By this feat of empathetic teleportation greater understanding is achieved of, for example, rubber-truncheon bearers. As Mrs Heathcote remarked at the Riverside conference: 'How do I get a delinquent to recognize a policeman's right to be more than a hunter?'

One sympathizes with anyone trying to arrange a friendly agreement between 'delinquents' and the police force, the material interests of these parties being so sharply opposed. In the part of London I live in, young blacks, who count as delinquents for police purposes, think the police have too many rights already. From their point of view, the police force is a criminal élite in uniform. Their attitude may strike some people as unfair, but it is not a million miles from Brecht's. This is not surprising, since Brecht was a poet of class struggle. Heathcote's reading of the poem represents *another* point of view.

Such is the fate of a statement launched from the particular to the universal. Upwards it zooms on its cosmic journey; one by one the specific factors which made it true in the first place detach and fall to earth; at last nothing is left but the hardware, quite neutral and blank, meaning more or less whatever one cares to make of it, burning itself up in endless circles.

DRAMA: A MATERIALIST VIEW

I've disagreed with two 'universal' statements at length to demonstrate the fact that disagreement is possible. They stand as what they are: expressions of opinion of neither more nor less value than any other until proved true or false. I think they are quite unsound; you may think they're true. That isn't the point. The point is that because they were plainly stated in a public address as they were at Riverside it is possible to register our agreement or scepticism in like terms.

However, Dorothy Heathcote's phrase 'from the particular to the universal' precisely describes the transformation undergone by a statement when, rather than being frankly articulated, it silently inhabits the ideology within which drama is taught. It is impossible to disagree with it – not because it is true, but because it has become invisible and untraceable.

Where is the student to detect it? At what point may he decide that what is universal for, say, the teacher, is not universal for him?

When, in the drama class, no structure of objective fact is used as a term of reference, or the ideological nature of the context remains unrecognized, the dangers are these: that opinion takes on the appearance of absolute truth; that the subjective experiences of the students, however influenced by the school setting (let alone by the banalities of television and home life) are given a moral weight they don't deserve; and that rational dissent against prevailing ideas is neither trained, nor, where it struggles into life, faced with a tangible opponent.

The pervading image becomes that of society which is constant, absolute, but flawed.

The teaching then becomes remedial; not of the student, but of society. The student is taught to make the best of this world, to correct the faults it produces, but not to transform the forces which produce those faults. The concept of an absolute and constant world full of universal truths is reinforced: the understanding of its relative nature, of the fact that it is the consequence of specific historical conflicts, is weakened.

Drama activities based on subjective experience, absolute truth and unchallengeable morality may be applied to real social situations in the hope that this will give the exercise some meaning for the group. For example, a common theme of classroom drama is racial prejudice often leading, in improvisation, to violence. But when approached simply on the subjective level of feelings, intuitions, or from the idea that it is all caused by 'lack of understanding' this can very easily teach,

quite inaccurately, that the roots of racial violence are psychological, neurotic or crass, and that economic, cultural and
political factors are nothing to do with it. If the teacher feels that
a 'political' point must be found, there's nothing to stop him
doing so. However, he will have to produce it out of his hat.
And what will it be? Probably that, 'it's the fault of the system'.
The *drama* exercise promptly loses whatever point it had, since
the 'system' is quite immune against examination by such means.
An ambush of snowballs would be more effective.

A vast amount of literature exists – books, pamphlets, independent newspapers – which approaches racial violence (and unemployment, and housing etc., etc.) in *material* terms. Facts,
figures and (given luck and care) political analysis can quite
easily be found and provided by the teacher for the class. It's
when material ammunition of this kind is at hand for the study of
social problems – rather than just the subjective experiences of
happiness, helplessness, empathy or mistrust – that students begin
to be armed against the mystifications of ideology, and can begin
to decide for themselves whether these 'problems' are in fact
problems at all, and, if so, what they can do about them.

As demonstrations were once described as 'rehearsals for the
revolution', so can the drama class be a rehearsal for the demonstration. Political action demands many of the same skills of the
activist as drama claims to teach: articulacy, insight, an ability to
work with others. The study even of a hypothetical political
action in the school, or out of the school, immediately throws up
problems which *again* can be the subject of drama work. How
does one proceed? By stealth? By aggression? How do we articulate our aims? How do we win support? One of the fields of
drama is the study of people in action. Where this is political
action, the work of the drama class can be based on imagination,
theory, and practice too.

Activities like this will very likely be limited by the school.
When this is so, a useful lesson can be learnt about the nature of
the school itself; and this again is a lesson well suited to study in
the drama class.

It's unfortunate that in any discussion involving authority,
unhelpful moral overtones will accrue. There's also a problem
when discussing ideology: the assumption that dominant beliefs
so condition people's minds that they become incapable of
working out alternatives.

It by no means follows from anything I've said that the drama teacher is a mere helpless prop of our social system. On the contrary, I hope these observations will be useful to drama teachers who see their work as more dynamic than that.

FORM AS MATERIALISM

Can the practices of theatre be helpful to drama teachers? In the sixties, drama teachers largely abandoned theatre in a reaction against the uncomprehending recitation of texts and received notions of what theatrical performances are and can be. It may now be clear that I am arguing against the consequent jettisoning of form in drama work, and against what I regard as a deluded reliance on subjective experience.

In the theatre, form is used as a way of isolating arguments and presenting them for scrutiny. I suggest that form in the drama lesson can serve the same function. This affects the whole issue of whether drama exercises should be 'performed' by one half of the class to the other. I'm suggesting that they should: that this is where examination of whatever issue is the subject of the exercise can start.

Earlier I noted three features of theatre as an art form: each is a limitation of the form in which the statement of the play is made, and together they combine to give it a certain *relative* quality. Even if that statement is partly concealed, as is usually the case in bourgeois theatre, is is possible to decode it. Once extracted, it stands revealed, not alone, but in relation to its formal context: a certain space, a certain duration, a certain concept of the world.

The last proviso is crucial: the argument of the play is not ideal; it might be true only in the specific set of social, economic and cultural circumstances revealed and implied in the play. It is, in this sense, objective; it is relative; and it is refutable. It is, if you like, particular. But it is not universal.

(I am grateful to David Lan for a number of valuable suggestions at an early stage in the writing of this chapter.)

5. Theatre for Young People
Gerald Chapman with John Dale

What has a child meant when, entering the Royal Court, he or she has turned to the teacher and asked, 'Am I wearing the right clothes, Miss?', or when another has said after the performance, 'Not as good as our drama, Miss!' or, more devastatingly, 'It wasn't real, it was *theatrical*'? We all like to think that the theatre holds a mirror up to nature. Is the mirror distorted, therefore, and if so, who is doing the distorting? These questions concerning the relationship between theatre and social reality are being confronted by a great many theatre groups in a variety of ways. Some, like Peter Brook's International Centre for Theatre Research, travel across deserts in search of answers; some, like Welfare State, set fire to the sea or even travel under it in a submarine[1]; some others are content to

> Look sometimes at
> The theatre whose stage is the street.[2]

When a child says of a play, 'it wasn't real it was theatrical', it is the whole of theatre, not simply the one play which is in the dock. Equally, this child's own kind of theatre, in or out of school, has come under attack recently for much the same reasons. While some teachers do not allow theatricality to sully the precious reality of their drama lesson, theatre people – especially managements – remain oblivious of the true quality of children's drama, preferring to treat young people simply to regular doses of the 'magic of the theatre'. This magic has worn pretty thin: a young audience used to the sophistication of TV and cinema is unlikely to be taken in any more by a few tricks. It is time for us magicians in the theatre to hang up our toppers and learn afresh our duties to this young and, as we have seen, accusing audience.

This chapter tries to confront the child's accusation from the point of view of one theatrical institution only – The Young People's Theatre Scheme at the Royal Court Theatre in London.

WHY GO TO THE THEATRE?

The Royal Court has traditionally been in the vanguard of contemporary theatre. Seventy years ago, the J. E. Vedrenne/ Harley Granville-Barker management pursued an aggressively forward-thinking policy, launching the plays of Shaw as well as Granville-Barker himself. In 1955, the English Stage Company leased the theatre and we were poised for that dramatic and irreversible shift in sensibility which accompanied the first production of *Look Back in Anger*. The shock was profound. Characteristically, society hit back by labelling subsequent moves to depict the grim realities of contemporary culture 'Kitchen-Sink Drama'. Intended as a snobbish rebuke, this became quite a precise definition to guide unsuspecting patrons to or away from the theatre. But the Artistic Director, George Devine, abhorred such categorizations and followed a broad-based policy of presenting different kinds of plays embracing all of Polonius' famous definitions. He was not interested in a special kind of play but rather in a special kind of experience in which a 'truly educated and critical audience [could], in a non-didactic way, ... share a common feeling with the artists of the theatre'.[3] Devine is here defining a theatre of integrity. He formulated the following list of basic questions:

> Why go to the theatre?
> What has it to do with me?
> What should I look for?
> How should I look?
> How should I listen?
> Is there theatre in life? How? Where?
> What sort of experience should I expect of the theatre?

The insistence on the first person singular emphasizes his belief in the [personal commitment and identification needed to make art meaningful.] Devine wanted to create 'a free and compulsive quality [in drama] not as an adjunct to literature but as a special kind of experience, which could relate art to its time and the human condition'. The way he faced this challenge was boldly imaginative, anticipating developments in community theatre and T.I.E. by several years. He wanted trained actors in schools, factories, polytechnics and education colleges; short films and publications containing relevant information about the productions so as to set up new critical approaches; regular opportunities for the audience to meet the actors socially; competitions in dramatic criticism and theatre photography; even 'ambassadors' sent to the provinces with 'the express purpose of lifting the lid off the so-called mystery of the contemporary theatre'. Above all there was to be the Studio, a research establishment that consisted of a congregation of different artists experienced in mime, movement, painting and music as well as acting – a 'Bauhaus of the Theatre' working full-time and devoted to two principal aims. First, 'to produce the nucleus of highly skilled actors for the Court or anyone else' – a new kind of actor to express the new kind of drama, that 'special kind of experience'. Second, to run workshops for anyone who wanted to join in, but particularly for children. Devine had already begun 'a series of researches' with senior school children; now the Studio began working with infants, four years old, producing participation plays with complete collaboration between actors and audience.[4]

The Studio clearly established the primacy of creative expression on the part of children; it gave them an equal voice with the actor; it did not hinder them with any preconceptions about who should be doing the acting and who should be watching it. To drama teachers, this situation is perfectly familiar: in fact it is a pre-requisite for the lesson because only when a child can experience something in drama *and* be able to reflect on it simultaneously can there be true learning. In the theatre (where economic factors also intrude), this kind of integrated experience is very rare.[5] The polarization of artists and audience was exactly what Devine strove to break down and in 1962 he correctly predicted exactly where the process should begin: 'I am deeply and entirely convinced that the solution lies in the schools and a radical re-appraisal of the teaching of drama'.

These re-appraisals have already begun, as other chapters in this book testify, and the great T.I.E. movement has helped to consolidate the new philosophies that have emerged from first-class teachers. These philosophies have themselves been tested and proven by the increasing political sophistication of the most forward-thinking theatre groups, some of which emerged out of the student maelstrom of the late 1960s.[6]

Now, over a decade later, it is possible to see just how momentous a movement for change these activities were. For the first time in three centuries, since the iron (safety) curtain fell on the first proscenium arch stage rigidly separating those who are paid to do from those who pay to watch, the theatre is exploding out of the traditional confines of building and training, and into the community, schools and clubs, into new kinds of actors and drama teachers. However, this theatrical revolution gives no cause for complacency. Local authorities are still largely philistine or snobbish towards the arts. Vocational drama schools remain largely oblivious of T.I.E. and Community work. The New Applications Committee continues to command a pitifully small vote within the Arts Council's budget. Nevertheless, despite the initial misunderstandings and hostility between drama teachers and theatres while first principles on either side were being worked out, there now exists as never before a climate of potential cooperation that could begin to fulfill Devine's vision of a radical theatre which integrated actors and audience alike in 'a special kind of experience', and so begin to answer those seminal questions which began, 'why go to the theatre?'.

THEATRE FOR YOUNG PEOPLE AND THE ROYAL COURT

The Schools Scheme which Devine's successor, William Gaskill, set up in 1966, (eventually known as the Young People's Theatre Scheme) was central to the rationale of the Court's existence, at a time when it was the most influential theatre in the western world. If, as Devine prophesied, 'the solution lies in the schools', then the relationship between the Y.P.T.S. and the Court (and between any Y.P.T. and its parent theatre) is a good barometer of how far the theatre as a whole is fulfilling its function.

However radical or innovative theatre work may be, it will always be the province of a privileged minority unless and until we can make it accessible to children and young adults, who are in an unique position to judge the culture bequeathed to them because they have fewer vested interests. If in the long term a theatre's effectiveness in society can only be measured by its provision for children, it follows that Y.P.T. should be in the vanguard of a theatre's policy. There are, however, many

practical and professional problems in the way of effective co-
operation between Theatre and Education.

The stormy histories of a lot of Y.P.T. and T.I.E. groups
(the Y.P.T.S included) testify to this. Differences of pay for
Equity members and those on the Burnham scale have hampered
co-operation between L.E.A.'s and their local theatres. Some
enlightened L.E.A.'s, perhaps exasperated by a theatre's failure to
respond to young people, have set up their own teams of actor-
teachers. Other T.I.E. groups have been forced to divorce themselves from their parent theatres and become independent simply
because their survival was threatened by the theatres' chipping
away at their budget and morale, forcing ideological differences
into the open. T.I.E. and community groups rightly clamour for
status and priority funding from public bodies and often despise
established theatres which, they claim, only serve about three per
cent of the population while *they* strive to make contact with the
ninety-seven per cent. The confusion and anger are bitter because
time and time again the mainstream theatre's attitude is that
Y.P.T. work, however successful or innovatory, is really only
ancillary to the main work and therefore dispensable when times
are hard. Behind this stance is the whole edifice of divisive social
attitudes which treat children as second-class citizens.

One of the reasons why the Royal Court Y.P.T.S. has survived
this attrition is that it has always been part of the libertarian
tradition of the theatre. The first two directors of the Y.P.T.S.,
Jane Howell and then Pam Brighton, were both in sympathy
with the Court's function, and were both protégées of the
Artistic Director at the time, William Gaskill, himself a colleague
of Devine and a veteran fighter against theatre censorship.
Moreover the Y.P.T.S. has always been independent of the Inner
London Education Authority and this has proved to be a crucial
factor on a number of occasions. The most famous of these was
the furore caused by Pam Brighton's production in 1970 of *The
Sport of my Mad Mother* by Ann Jellicoe. Some of the language
had been altered or adapted into a more contemporary style,
much in the way that teachers have often updated old classics in
order to make their themes more accessible to children. The
irony was neat. Here was a play from the Court's 1958 season
which had flopped but which had become a modern classic and
was adopted as an examination set-text. If proof were needed of
the success of Devine's bold policy this was it. But the I.L.E.A.

were outraged by the swear words. Questions about the squandering of public money and corruption of children's morals were asked in the House of Commons. The Court rallied behind the Y.P.T.S. and remained staunchly supportive of its 'Youth Section'. Many other examples exist of public outcry or local authority harrassment in this field, and it seems clear that since censorship was abolished in 1968 the political cutting-edge in theatre now belongs almost exclusively to young people's work. This is partly a symptom of how the arts in general have been emasculated, their power to disrupt decanted off into the correspondence columns of the Times Literary Supplement.

Between 1972 and 1976 the Y.P.T.S. Director was Joan Mills. A recruit from Hull University's drama department and with some direct teaching experience, her training represented precisely the source of hope in British Theatre which Devine had been striving for ten years earlier. As such her's seemed a shrewd appointment on the part of Oscar Lewenstein, the Artistic Director, and he nurtured her with great love and care in the unfamiliar jungle of theatre politics (and Royal Court politics at that) in which she now found herself. There was a dramatic change of policy. The slightly chaotic, though inspired, approach of Pam Brighton was replaced with a carefully articulated bias towards educational drama which Mills wanted to fulfil through the establishment of London's fourth T.I.E. team.

By 1975, however, with no proper administrative structure for the Y.P.T.S., and without the necessary confidence of the management in support of her ideas, Mills found herself increasingly isolated. In the past it had always been one person's responsibility to encourage and cajole directors and other members of staff to take an interest in educational activities. This was even the case under Devine when it was Keith Johnstone's knack of persuasion that resulted in the week-long courses for dozens of children which involved Gaskill, Devine himself or Tony Richardson. John Dexter would be asked to show kids the fly-gallery and would shin up the ladders after them; Miriam Brickman would answer the questions of fifteen third years crammed into her tiny Casting Director's office; and Johnstone himself would take a class to a wrestling match as an example of 'theatre in life'. None of these activities could ever have become a regular occurrence, as both Jane Howell and Pam Brighton were to discover: the disruption to the hectic routine was too great. A lot depended, therefore, on the efficiency of the Y.P.T.S.'s administrative relationship to the theatre, and with one person trying to do everything *and* trying to introduce some unfamiliar ideas it was unlikely that Mills would be in for a smooth ride. Nevertheless the theatre was supportive in some surprising ways, not least when, in a desperate bid to make up for the anticipated loss on Peter Gill's celebrated production of Edward Bond's *The Fool*, it chose to shut down the Theatre Upstairs, rather than the Y.P.T.S. Ironically, this hugely controversial action allowed the Y.P.T.S. the facility to use the Theatre Upstairs more extensively than it had ever done before, and several writers came and took workshops for children including Bond himself!

At this time the economy was in a shambles and the education cuts were under way. But even if Joan Mills had been given her T.I.E. team by the I.L.E.A. (to whom she appealed in vain), she failed to gain the credibility of a theatre that did not value what she was doing. The Court was not interested in educational 'processes' that seemed too abstract, too little related to social realities. In despair she resigned, and there was a three month gap before someone else was appointed. All the many close ties she had forged with individual schools over three and a half years were lost; the youth theatre group she had run splintered; the budget had become run down; the mailing list was in a confusing mess; the Y.P.T.S. committee became even more toothless than before; even the idea of the Young Writers Festival, a conspicuously successful invention of her regime, was in danger of being lost to the National Theatre. In short the Y.P.T.S. policy quickly disintegrated as the commitment of a particular individual withdrew. But there was no solid administrative basis on which the policy *could* survive. Were it not for the particular interest of the two Co-Artistic Directors, Robert Kidd and Nicholas Wright, and of one particular Council of Management member, Edward Blacksell, the Y.P.T.S. could quite easily have been killed off. Many a regional theatre has effected such a murder of its Y.P.T. company. Not until 1979 did the Court manage to revive the Y.P.T.S. sufficiently so as to guarantee its future efficacy. In that year it was employing a full time administrative and artistic staff of four people, not just one, solitary whizz-kid. Once more the Court was responding not just to a single part, but to its *total* function as a theatre.

This story illustrates yet again the crucial relationship between a Y.P.T. company and its parent theatre; the strength of either can only be diminished by a policy of divide and rule. There is no particular virtue in the former going independent unless its departure provokes the latter seriously to re-think its overall function and to re-appraise its priorities in order to include a rigorous young people's policy. Unless theatres do this as a matter of urgency, they will be slowly replaced by the kitsch technological substitutes for art, conveniently packaged and literally dead safe. The signs are abundantly obvious: mass, technologically communicated, easily accessible culture in two centres of excellence, two mandarin palaces of pleasure that in 1977–78 commanded almost forty per cent of the *total* Drama allocation of the Arts Council.[7] And yet the number of plays that year which the National Theatre and the R.S.C. even defined as being especially for children could be counted on one hand. On top of this, the I.L.E.A. pours in thousands of pounds of extra subsidy to buy cheap tickets for matinee performances. Very worthy, but where is the rigour of it? And why and how do the children go along there? And is it 'real or theatrical'? Like a gaudy supermarket display, theatrical goods are thrust upon children like, 'the spectacle of plenitude behind plate glass, the clamour of competitive superlatives'.[8] Jeremy Seabrook's apt description of consumer-madness is sufficient warning for any theatre company tempted into superficial approaches to Young People's Theatre.

The Y.P.T.S. will always be a strange hybrid, yoked to many different forces that often want to drive it in conflicting directions. The local authority, the schools' staff, the Youth Service, the theatre management, parents, the Court's technical staff and not least the children themselves all influence the policy and to a greater or lesser extent (depending on the project) allow or disallow the work to be done. The Y.P.T.S. has decided to remain very flexible in its areas of concern, sticking its fingers into almost every conceivable pie as a matter of choice. This allows one to make some unconventional connections, linking professionals and amateurs in surprising, creative liaisons. There may not be a single linear direction to the work, but a complex of relationships can still harbour an overall aim. This is embedded in the question, 'What is it like to be young today?' It was armed with this 'policy-question' that, as the next Y.P.T.S. director, I went out and talked to teachers.

MAKING CONNECTIONS

For about a week after I arrived I felt I could do without teachers; 'such a boring lot', I was told, and not being teacher-trained I was inclined to agree. My impression of a flimsy form of improvisation which passed for drama did not fire any enthusiasm for formal educational contacts and, like so many theatre professionals, I arrogantly assumed I could conveniently ignore the education establishment. The attitude of the Court itself was to delegate; 'You are, after all, the expert', said Stuart Burge, the Artistic Director, later on in 1977.

Following the advice of an ex-teacher friend, I ventured to talk to a drama advisor who put me on to a 'hot list' of twelve very good drama teachers. One by one, I interviewed each of them, following up two or three more contacts from each person. My prejudice and naiveté quickly became replaced by an admiration and a sympathy for what these fine teachers were doing and within four months I had already conceived the skeletal structure of the conference from which this book springs.

I was impressed by the seriousness and integrity of the teachers' work, and especially by the fact that the children were here, at least, encouraged to possess their own art, to articulate their most powerful concerns and to create an image of society which could be judged by artists and audience alike. The common area of interest with the professional theatre was striking and yet the yawning gulf between the two disciplines pointed up the continual failures of the professional arts even to begin to address themselves to these concerns. The Y.P.T.S. has tried to rectify this by placing at the centre of our work the voice of the child and the image that is created from it: the emphasis is on children writing plays, or alternatively creating plays through improvisation. This is why, paradoxically, the Y.P.T.S. style of work approximates more closely to the professional discipline of a good drama teacher than the styles of T.I.E. or children's theatre companies which usually put less emphasis on children's own creativity, preferring to use drama as a more obviously pedagogic medium.

My feelings were going to be continually verified by the response of professional writers and directors who were put into close contact with youth or community groups; each time they were shocked and stimulated by the degree of cultural poverty children were oppressed with, and the passion with which children wanted to let others (especially of their own age) know about their feelings. Somehow the drama teachers' work, as anticipated by George Devine, held the clue to the way one creates a theatre of integrity.

However, this oppression of cultural poverty was soon to overwhelm our eagerness to please. Very quickly word got round that the Royal Court was offering help to teachers and, of course, it was the insecure teachers who were tripping over themselves in their conflicting demands. The Y.P.T.S. was treated as a teachers' panacea: advice on how to use the school hall for plays, advice on improvisation, demonstrations of make-up, visits round the theatre, advice on suitable scripts to use for a class of thirty girls in the first year, advice on multi-ethnic education, sexism, how to get children to write plays, how to produce *The Country Wife*, how to construct scenery, how to light a play with three lanterns, 'and what about the Cypriots? What are you going to do for them?' At this stage, I thought I was asking *them* for advice, attending teachers' courses and reading up on someone called Dorothy Heathcote whom everyone was invoking but of whom I had not even heard. The teachers were genuinely pleased, however, by the interest taken and the first season of the new regime was a resounding success. Only I.L.E.A.'s Drama Warden sounded a proper note of caution: *Inner London Education Authority*

> Some theatres try to create strong personal links with groups of young people – as, for instance, in the Royal Court's Y.P.T.S... But too often the impetus for this kind of work is from a particular individual's enthusism and commitment rather than as a vital part of theatre policy.[9]

The honeymoon was short-lived.

ENTHUSIASM, BIAS AND COMMITMENT

Part of the policy was to be seasons of plays on obviously social themes and the first of these provoked the biggest outcry since *The Sport of My Mad Mother*. Gay Sweatshop's play, *The Age of Consent*, for fifth and sixth years, was fully booked by teachers when a press campaign practically destroyed all the careful preparation. I.L.E.A. had lain low up until then, but felt obliged to join in the denunciation. The Press statements were revealing in their thinly disguised fear of the Arts as agents of real influence. After praising my intentions in wishing to promote greater understanding of, and tolerance for, homosexual people, the editor went on to denounce the use of drama as a way of exploring the issues:

> That means not only watching a play about a homosexual love affair, but also taking part in improvisations and role playing. A method that is admirably suited to creating understanding of many social problems. Sexual problems are not among them. They are too explosive. For teenagers they need to be handled in a lower key – not in drama but in discussion.[10]

Newspapers and TV programmes that comfortably deal with the scientific complexities of moon-shots, re-entry procedures and fast-breeder reactors lack even a basic knowledge of an art-form whose expressive powers are available to everyone, even journalists of the popular press. Why is this so?

What the press condemned was the possibility of a personal and unsavoury identification between the children and the substance of the drama. Several papers, along with some teachers, accused me of deliberately raising the issue merely because I was gay myself. It seems that there are some social issues which are only acceptable to the press and the public for as long as they can believe that no-one is really involved in them.

Teachers will tell you how difficult it was until quite recently to commit schools to a policy of multi-cultural education. Now there are L.E.A. papers on it and the whole subject is thoroughly *de rigeur*. Even so, one teacher, whose drama club is sixty per cent West Indian, has been accused of favouritism because the school itself is only thirty per cent West Indian. This is racist cant, but it illustrates the suspicion of personal commitment which drama teachers in particular seem to suffer from. Drama, being the most social of the arts, very obviously exposes the personal commitment (or lack of it) of the artist.[11] What more effective way of 'protecting' the child from adverse influence than barring him or her access to the personal enthusiasm (translated into 'bias') of a committed adult?

And yet individual opinions are supposed to be honoured in school. Free expression is a pre-requisite of the humanities . . . is it not?

If teachers are caught on the horns of a dilemma, we can only guess how much more confused children are likely to be by the hypocrisy of a society that teaches one thing and practises something else. For it is clear that outside multi-cultural schooling, it is not such a safe thing to be black, nor is a sixteen-year-old's political opinion worth much to our vaunted Parliamentary democracy . . . the list of examples is endless, a list of powerlessness, of personal enthusiasm being translated into personal failure.

Drama can disrupt because there is a personal engagement between the artist's own individuality and what is being portrayed. Ian McKellen has spoken of fulfilling his 'potential for murder' by playing Macbeth. Likewise a good maths teacher brings to the teaching of numeracy the necessary (and personal) concern for paying the rent. These equations between personal involvement and the public's need are important ones and ensure the effectiveness and *affectiveness* of both acting and teaching. To discredit personal bias is to trivialize such equations, and it is a common enough weapon. In recent years the personal bias of all teachers, but particularly of those who do not sit comfortably in the utilitarian juggernaut of contemporary society, has been increasingly called into question. Cultural poverty is itself the result of the powerlessness of most teachers as well as the children, to solve the contradictions they encounter daily. One teacher, referring to the Riverside Conference, put it succinctly by referring back to everyone's own experience of being taught:

> Most disturbing was the statement: 'The biggest problem of teachers is that they view from doubt.' Very true, and it hit home; and made me very aware of the insecurity felt by most teachers. . . . It is not just teachers who view from doubt. Teachers *are viewed* from doubt. All of us have had experiences of bad teachers, simply through having been at school.

Personal bias is a catalyst (and a very necessary one) which allows one to act or to teach in such a way as to confront social contradictions, and by confronting them to effect some commitment to change. Because Arts Education aims more directly than the professional arts to confront these contradictions as they impinge on the awareness of the growing child, it invites more public scorn from reactionary forces. In the long term this may well make Arts Education practitioners more vulnerable, more cautious and ultimately more conventional than their colleagues in the professional arts. On top of this, educationalists have to cope with poor facilities, a weighty bureaucracy, oversized classes and an examinable curriculum in the forty or fifty minute periods allocated perhaps once or twice a week. No director would tolerate an infernal bleeping noise to interrupt rehearsals. The whole concept of time allowed for arts activity changes as soon as one leaves the school building. And even if teachers take children out of school to the theatre, the transport problems of a huge city quickly dampen one's enthusiasm.[12]

MAKING CONTACT

By 1978, the Y.P.T.S. had done substantial work with groups of West-Indians, gays, Bengalis, truants, Indians and indeed even some Glaswegians; seminars on politics, writers' workshops and a variety of professional productions had all been on offer. Yet teachers were not booking; they had forgotten their own enthusiasm of two years before. The conflicting responses this time were: staff cuts make it impossible; pressure of exam syllabus; why do you only appeal to clever kids?; broaden your programme; narrow your programme; 'we haven't forgotten that gay business'; no money; the leaflet was too large to photo-copy; did not see the back of the leaflet; have not read the leaflet; no time; no time; no time. . . . These were the 'resounding tinkles' of confusion, doubt and failure. When one teacher added, 'And what about the Cypriots? What have you done for them?' it seemed like the time to turn to Stuart Burge and say, 'I am not an expert any more. These people really are boring!' Of course the elephantine bureaucracy and hard toil of the teaching profession are tailor-designed to frustrate the most radical attempts of those involved in Arts Education. Just as a theatre is tempted not to bother about the kids, so a school is tempted not to bother about outside agencies unless they clearly slot into the needs of the syllabus. The Y.P.T.S., with its emphasis on extra-curricular as well as cross-curricular activity, can hardly compete in such circumstances with subsidized schools' matinees at the National Theatre, *Grease* or disco night at the Lyceum. It can no more answer the question, 'What are you going to do for the Cypriots?' than can the I.L.E.A.'s Inspectorate for Social Studies or any other studies.

What is the solution to this problem of relating to teachers? Just as the Y.P.T.S. gives children the voice to create their image of society through play-making, so with teachers it is trying to let them reclaim a power that is rightly theirs. This in practice has led to the forming of a Teachers Policy Group, open to anyone, meeting fortnightly and being encouraged to be as responsible as the theatre for the success or failure of the Y.P.T.S. No longer should one depend on whim alone in booking events but on a mutual planning – the sharing of opinions on scripts which can then be studied by classes in advance, the yoking of productions to teachers' conferences on particular topics, the involvement of actors in the classroom work of the teacher prior to the teacher's involving the class in the theatre-craft of the actors. This is not an unobtainable ideal; there are many examples of it already in T.I.E. This provision of time for present reflection before future commitment is a political as well as aesthetic need: if theatre and education adequately reflect today, then their mutual reflection will help create tomorrow. But there must be a proper understanding of their different but complementary powers so that crude misuse of one party by the other can be replaced by respect for their true value and contribution.

The complex relationships between Y.P.T. work, a parent theatre and the limitless number of organizations and individuals that officially or unofficially service youth testify to the need for flexibility in one's approach, exploiting the possibilities, and at the same time holding firmly on to certain principles that define one's relationship with young people themselves. In the case of the Y.P.T.S. these principles are:

1. Giving young people the power to voice their concerns. Theatre has a unique capacity to achieve this.
2. Giving young people the confidence that their voice is (a) worth listening to, and (b) will be heard properly. This means being a good audience by 'sharing a common feeling with the artists'.

In pursuing these basic principles we have developed work in four main areas: 1. Encouraging young people's writing for the theatre; 2. Community youth theatre shows; 3. Workshops with professional writers; 4. The Royal Court Youth Theatre club, the Activists.

YOUNG WRITERS

The Y.P.T.S. runs its own annual Young Writers Festival. Started by Joan Mills in 1973 from a suggestion of Nicholas Wright's (the Theatre Upstairs Artistic Director at the time), it quickly became a popular event which critics and audiences alike found refreshingly original, partly because the plays were relatively unsophisticated and raw in their vision of life, partly because it easily invited a paternalistic response which glamourized the four or five young writers at the expense of the 250 others whose work had not been chosen for production. The voice which sounds most insistently in all this vast outpouring of children's writing every year is a bleak and often extremely violent one. The prevailing tone is one of failure and self-oppression, or alternatively, of criminal desperation:[13]

> Since I damn well left school two years ago nothing's come my way. Only achievement, except being an apprentice mechanic – dropped that – was being a guest in Her Majesty's nick. Left that a week ago; wish I hadn't. I felt more with myself – with people I know did nearly the same thing I did. I'm alone now. Don't know what to do now. But Babylon ain't gonna stop me stealing them, mugging 'em and raping 'em, no Sir! No Sir! 'Cause I'm still a qualified stamped and tested school leaver and where it get me? (The lights slowly fade down while everyone on the stage is frozen. As the lights fade Peter Tosh's 'Get Up, Stand Up for Your Rights' is played.)[14]

A great deal of classroom drama deals in media clichés adapted particularly from television soap operas. The alleged truth of an improvisation based on the nexus Mum-Dad-Homework-TV is often to an outsider, an apparent confirmation of class stereotypes, an expert portrayal of how life really is at the tea-table for these children. A good teacher knows that it is a sham, a dazzling, synthetic lie, partly because the attitudes adopted in such work never threaten to upset the *status quo* of the children who enact them, however extreme they may appear to be. When we say we prefer children to write 'from their own experience' we are asking them to reflect on that experience at the same time so that the situations they write about can be understood *and* judged to be valid. That is a very difficult thing to do and it is no surprise to learn that many of the entries we receive for the Festival are actually fulfilling other demands imposed upon them by media images and the received concepts of proper language. Patois is outlawed in schools because it threatens the status of the Queen's English, and the demotic versions of even that are outlawed, blue-pencilled for being obscene. Four-letter words may just be OK in the privacy of the drama studio but they are not OK in the public arena. The result is often antiseptically written plays or good clean fun in youth theatre performances.[15]

The entries for the Young Writers Festival, therefore, bear witness to a complex process of intimidation and cultural deprivation which at its most extreme form results in an idealization of the very forces which intimidate. There is glamour in militarism, in uniforms, in the persecution of innocent victims, and in suppression of vandals. A recurring motif in the playscripts we receive is the school being burnt down deliberately, and the police then being telephoned so that a cops and robbers style chase can be contrived with the children acting out their Steve McQueen fantasies. In court the characters plead all the usual mitigating factors (unemployment, broken homes, poverty, lack of education). The play then reaches its dénouement with the ultimate cliché solution: the judge and police officers are either shot dead and the defendant runs away or alternatively (and more often) the judge condemns the defendant to death. In one play, a whole class of pupils, who had done no more than stage a sit-in to protest against the raising of the school leaving age to nineteen, were lined up and executed. In either case, real justice seems unobtainable and satisfaction is only gained by at once idealizing authority figures and rendering them murderers.[16] In drama lessons, as in writing plays, one is concerned with isolating those points where decisions, whether in fantasy or not, are no longer tested by reality. Where in this saga of Mum-Dad-Homework-TV or schools being burnt down and cops and robbers car chases can one locate the moments when dramatic truth or mendacity hang in the balance? What Heathcote and Bolton and Gaskill were doing at Riverside was trying to answer that question as precisely as possible. They did it by questioning the automatic, habitual response to reality in order to deepen perception of that reality, whether on the part of the child, the actor or the audience. Both the children's and the actors' memories were invoked in order to help evaluate a dramatic situation. In our cops and robbers play the flight into fantasy at the end is not *in itself* a dramatic cop-out. What is crucial is that the confrontation between *the need for justice and the way justice is effected* needs to be clear. Most of the plays don't display this clarity because adult society itself smudges the issue; children swiftly learn that their firm concepts of fairness, often strongest at the age of eleven or twelve, will not be adequate whether in or out of school. The despairing cry of Errol at the end of *The School Leaver* amply demonstrates this loss of innocence, and, for him, the determination to engage in crime follows quite logically. This is no media cliché; the author is actually saying something very radical, asking us not so much to judge Errol (because Errol is already judged and convicted) but to judge a situation. And it is because we know that there are so many Errols in existence that we can test our judgement not against the private concerns of a writer but against our knowledge of society. So much drama, whether on TV, in the classroom or in script form, fails this test.[17] Drama is sometimes seen as a sop to soak up idle people in their increased leisure-time, so that they can 'express themselves' in some form of remedial compensation, some form of mild palliative. Violent or apathetic teenagers, unemployed or depressed, are eagerly exploited by well-meaning drama tutors, but the work so often fails because the actual personalities of these people are submerged.

Too often children are not taken seriously by the arts; nor often enough, by schools. Rather they either become a stimulus for smug educational cant that smothers their identity in a welter of jargon. Or, alternatively the response to children acting out their own plays (or the plays of adults) is often, 'Well, I'm sure they get a lot out of it' or, more rudely, 'But who's it for?' Many school productions or youth club improvisations are actually set up merely to satisfy such criteria. Quality of content and dynamic communication with an audience are sacrificed for an easy compromise, perhaps full of energy but completely lacking in any cutting edge. Children and teachers assiduously wield the Leichner and flick the dimmers but the pageant remains resolutely insubstantial. The current suspicion of quality in youth theatre or young people's writing (neither of which have glamour or box-office appeal) is shared by professional theatre-workers and educationalists. Children are just not expected to achieve high standards.

There are two instances of Y.P.T.S. youth theatre productions which have crossed the accepted boundaries, and disrupted the

Professional/Amateur *status quo*. The first, Pam Brighton's celebrated Sunday-night production in 1971 of Harold Mueller's *Big
Wolf*, was a play about teenage war-orphans, inspired by
Vietnam. The young cast, drawn from local schools, brought to
the play a devastating authenticity. The script had been gathering
dust for some time, before Brighton discovered it; Gaskill
immediately scheduled it for professional production in the main
theatre the following spring. But the young professionals, all in
their early twenties, failed to match the passionate engagement of
their teenage counterparts. Gaskill then asked the kids to recreate
their performance (dormant for several months) in front of a
desultory cast at the other end of a bleak rehearsal room. Mueller
witnessed this impromptu performance and he later claimed it to
be the best production of his play in England or Germany.

The second example is the 1977 Activists' Youth Theatre Club
production of *Spring Awakening*, directed by Tim Fywell and
John Chapman. Film producers, TV directors, actors, casting
directors and the Court's own artistic hierarchy joined the mums,
dads and friends of the cast in the tiny disused garage behind
Sloane Square underground station where it was performed. It
was not only that a particularly high standard was achieved, it
was that the force of children's creative imagination was
revealed in a context which was generally regarded as the
province of the National Theatre or R.S.C. – the classic revival.
The production also triumphantly vindicated what Irving
Wardle describes as Devine's Law: 'that theatrical impact is an
equation between what happens and where it happens.'[1] The
political potential of the school play (where adults, including
perhaps the school governors, are obliged to listen to kids for a
change instead of vice versa) can so often be destroyed by a
cruelly patronizing carelessness. Similarly the actual conditions
under which drama lessons are taught can insidiously undermine
a sense of purpose and pride. One lesson I attended was
continually interrupted by the schoolkeepers' clomping right
through the middle of the drama hall: the teacher and her class
did not seem to mind, inured as they were to this kind of brutal-
ization of the privacy and concentration necessary to honour the
child's creativity and of the teacher's dignity to be able to respond
to it. Nevertheless, what the class was actually learning about
was the unchallenged power of the schoolkeepers' mentality, and
a whole cycle of repression was thus built into the lesson. We

may be teaching tolerance and understanding but do we really listen?

The importance of the Young Writers Festival is not that four children are bright enough to get their plays done professionally (that is the media response) but that they are claiming for themselves the right for their own Art to be seen and, therefore communicated freely to others, whether they are actors or audience. Other children claim that right through graffiti. In either case, the Art is centred on the reality of children's lives and is deliberately, systematically executed.[19]

'Graffiti Theatre', to coin a phrase, depends on the clear and daring outbursts of individuals fashioned into an art-form that is not necessarily based on narrative or characterization. It derives its strength from the hold on our curiosity of what ordinary people have to say about themselves. *The Iceman Cometh*, *Kennedy's Children*, *Chorus Line*, *Word Is Out*, or *For Coloured Girls Who Have Considered Suicide When The Rainbow Is Enuf* are all celebrated American examples of Graffiti Theatre (or in one case, film). The success of *Runaways*, which was about children and performed by them even on Broadway, shows that you don't have to be alcoholic, a dancer or a member of an oppressed minority group to qualify for this treatment. Nor does Graffiti Theatre eschew the writer's craft in favour of random monologues. What is distinctive is the quality of listening which is required.

COMMUNITY YOUTH THEATRE

There is nothing random in the way the Y.P.T.S. chooses the groups of young people it wants to work with on a community show. On the surface it seems as though the choice of Bengalis in the East End, truants in Barking, Indians in Tooting, West Indians in Portobello Road and gays from all over London is merely a tokenist stance, designed *pour épater les bourgeois*. The fact is, of course, that each of these groups have got something very particular they want to say. Each has been badly hurt – many of them physically as well as emotionally. Nowhere is the confrontation between 'the need for justice and the way justice is effected' more clearly demonstrated than with groups such as these. Society's own balancing act between truth and mendacity uses minority groups as its treadwire. As a result, theatre is at its most effective in confronting an audience with an unfamiliar or uncomfortable truth by deliberately forcing open those doors which have hitherto been slammed against such groups through ignorance or prejudice. Racial or sexual prejudice operates by denying its victims their basic humanity and seeks to obliterate their very existence either by deporting, imprisoning or 'curing' them. In the case of the gay teenagers, the law relating to the age of consent threatens their freedom if they assert their sexuality at a time when it is most important to them, when it defines their social identity. The door which this play forced open, therefore, revealed no more than simply the sight of eight young men and women proclaiming their sexuality, but in so far as it could easily have incurred legal sanction, such a moving proclamation also became a piece of political action. The drama lay in the fleshing out, literally, of the legend that is never scrawled on a concrete wall:

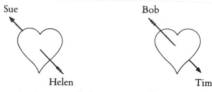

MARK: If someone's damaged, he covers that part of him up. Like a wound or a sore. If you make someone feel damaged, he covers himself up. We could all be walking round with wounds and sores and no-one would know that we were no different, no worse, because we'd all be hiding. We're covered up people. Nobody knows that we're here. One in twenty people is gay. Maybe more. Every time twenty people are collected together, it's likely that one of them is gay. Five per cent. In this country three million people at least. Men and women. Where do they come from? From us. Nobody knows we exist. We do. We're not worse. We are different. Who isn't? We don't want you to do anything. Some of us want to change the world. Some of us don't. We work. We think. We talk. We listen. We play. But nobody knows that we're here. We're not asking you to do anything special. We just want you to know. We don't want to be covered up people. We just want to tell you: We're here.[20]

To many people this simple truth is a bombshell and it forcefully illustrates the way theatre can so precisely reveal situation rather than just character.

In Brick Lane, the act of theatre was prompted by daily assault and harassment.[21] It was this pressure which gave the Bengali play urgency, a sense of necessity. When people complain that this smacks of tub-thumping just ask them how often *they* have been beaten up in the streets. Extreme conditions require exacting solutions, and to oppose crude racist slogans with some Graffiti Theatre could be one of them.

WORKING WITH WRITERS

Working with these groups has usually involved a professional writer and director. We have yet to experiment with professional actors, although this is something which the Common Stock Theatre Company do frequently, culling material from the common stock of humanity, processing it through professional artistry, and finally representing it to community audiences. We feel there is an equal, if not greater, value in the groups' acting out for themselves their own reflections on something which is exclusively theirs. There are limitations in terms of acting ability and professional commitment, but the further away from source one moves the more open to misinterpretation one becomes. This is a fundamental problem for the theatre and the community theatre movement has only just begun addressing itself to it. It is not a question of bringing one's talents and culture to the attention of communities: rather it is wiping the slate clean and asking what is there in the communities that gives theatre urgency? For example, if this means temporarily ditching the very language one learnt at birth then one must ditch it and find another one. In the case of the Bengali and Indian groups the play was in a second language for them (i.e. English) because the language of their infancy had not yet adapted itself from classical myths and rituals into an appropriate medium for the expression of contemporary urban culture.

For a writer, having to find a new language can be a drastic enterprise. For some it means a change of role. David Lan who edited *Not in Norwich* for the gay group writes in the introduction to the play:

> The group consisted in the main of people with little or no experience as actors . . . to ask them to sustain a developed narrative and characterization would be too ambitious. It was necessary to

think about writing a play not only about them but also around them. . . . In the right circumstances they were all capable of mesmerizing everyone simply by talking about themselves. . . . The imaginative process of reconstruction, of memory and evaluation, became a primary act of creation. . . . The memory never lies. In its inaccuracies is found — if one learns to look for it — another very resonant kind of truth.

Leigh Jackson wrote *Aftermath* for the West Indian group but they found it impossible to act it out because they could not read well enough to learn the lines. For the Bengali play, *East End on Lakeland*, Dilip Hiro wrote short scences interspersed with brief scenarios which were then improvised. During work on *Fuse* and *Playing the Flame* the Indian group yielded its own writer and in many ways this was the ideal solution. There is no guaranteed method. Nevertheless, the liaison between writer and group can be of mutual benefit.

So often writers, working in isolation, can lose touch with reality when it is actually their job to be thoroughly engaged with it. This temporary secondment enriches their awareness and so makes them better equipped professionally. Similarly when the writer helps a group of young people to analyse their private improvisations in order to make them publicly meaningful, this is the first step towards helping them become writers themselves. In the Young Writers' Workshops which we offer to people aged ten to twenty-three, this analysis can take many forms: observations of people in the street leading to monologues based on those characters; different sets of improvisations around one situation so as to reveal the different sets of logic that apply to the characters' behaviour. Edward Bond describes his workshop for young writers thus:

Good art is a combination of observation and analysis. The observation is necessary . . . to enable an audience to associate themselves with what is being shown. The analysis is necessary because this converts naturalism into realism, a record into art. . . . Alienation isn't the removal of an emotion, it is the adding of a commentary.

To teach these lessons I create difficulties for the participants — just as society creates difficulties for individuals. I make a girl tell about the loss of her child while she is preparing the cooking, or while she is working in a factory: it is necessary that she works, it is also necessary that she speaks honestly about her bereavment. Society does not regard her as an actress who can take ten minutes off for a dramatic solo. This situation must be made concrete in its social setting. . . .

Example of what not to do: in the theatre things happen in a room – this is wrong. Rooms have windows, people can live below and above. People talking in a room is naturalism. The room is in a house, the house is in a street, the street in a city, at the end of the street a prison, an H-Bomb site, a playground etc. Analysis: an individual can't tell you about himself by telling you about his soul. He tells you about himself by comparing himself with other people. . . . So we get away from showing the individual, not because he isn't important but because his situation must be analysed and this means showing social relationships.[22]

The Writers Workshops have revealed that:

1. It is actually possible to teach people how to write plays.
2. The socialization of the group, away from school routine and the presence of teachers, is crucial. Teachers are constantly surprised by (a) the quality of the group discussion, and (b) the quality of the writing.[23]
3. More time and small groups (i.e. ten people) are needed for this work. So far, the workshops have been for two days. We now plan to run longer courses including a weekly group that will meet for a whole year with an experienced writer.
4. Practical knowledge of the theatre is crucial. This means not only more theatre visits but the production of many more young playwrights' scripts. The Young Writers Festival is at present too random in the way it culls scripts; it should be linked to a systematic training for young writers.
5. This training doesn't depend on academic ability at all. It depends on the ability to understand one's social relationships. A group of very 'rough and unmotivated' third year pupils were once taken out of school every afternoon for two weeks to work with a writer and director. The report on this project details the slow but genuine progress towards getting the children to regard each other with greater understanding: 'What we achieved was probably not what we expected. We seem to have been a catalyst for the kids to express something to each other, rather than to us, especially across the sexual divide.'[24]

This ability to 'express something to each other' seems to us to be a prerequisite for a responsible society as well as for writing plays. In working with truants for almost a year, John Dale, the Assistant Y.P.T.S. Director, confronted this basic need to speak honestly (like Bond's example of the bereaved woman in the factory) and also the incredible difficulties that stood in the way of it. He had to gain their trust not as an artist, not as the funny man with the big nose, not as the serious man with the cassette recorder, but as a person who would listen, and all those other qualities were harnessed to that primary concern. Having been continually let down by authority, by family and by schooling some of them had developed a strong sense of independence which often masked a tremendous shyness. The urge to be patronizing whenever they laughed at him was great: 'How dare you laugh at me; I've come to help you!' These truants do not easily listen because others do not easily listen to them:

JOHN: So if you had a real problem, who would you go to?
CLIFF: No-one – I'd keep it to myself. If you keep your problems they just go eventually.
JOHN: Why is it important that your problems should be shown to other people?
SHARON: Well it has to be the right person. If it's someone who won't listen, you don't tell them do you.

One-to-one chats gradually built up enough trust for group work and then, quite suddenly, their energy was focused as they carefully transcribed and typed up the conversations before finally editing them into dramatic monologues. They never felt confident about acting them out before an audience, but they were happy to make the transcripts available to others, including writers, because they felt it might help other young truants:

DEBBIE: They listen to it and they might say, 'Oh well at least I'm not on my own'.
JOHN: What about adults, what do you think they might think of it?
DEBBIE: Probably think – stupid cow. I don't know really.[25]

Below John Dale gives an account of his more extensive contact with another kind of group.

The Royal Court Youth Theatre: 'The Activists'

Why should a theatre like the Royal Court, under constant financial pressure and the strain of atrocious facilities and appalling lack of space, take on the financial responsibility and time-consuming administrative problems of running a large Youth Theatre? If there is to be a Youth Theatre, then of what sort?

There are common misunderstandings about the nature of Youth Theatre Companies. A popular idea is that they exist to nurture the potential of young actors and actresses in the 'thespian art' before packing them off to make a fortune in films. Another is that a Youth Theatre is a bristling company of forty or more eager youngsters doing epic productions in modern dress of the crowd scenes from *Julius Caesar*. Perhaps most damaging, however, is the idea that Youth Theatre is really second-class stuff but that it's good to let the kids have a go and 'they're very good for their age'.

FIRST PRINCIPLES

The objectives of the Youth Theatre at the Royal Court reflect the general aims of the Y.P.T.S.

1. To give any young person the confidence to know that their voice is worth listening to.

This means that our company should be permanent and have an ever open door. Qualifications for the company are not acting ability or financial status but, quite simply, the amount of time the member is prepared to give and the desire to talk and share opinions. Many join out of a need for social contact with other young people and it is important to foster this social function: to encourage them to listen to each other and to create an equality within the group whatever their circumstances outside it.

2. To give power and status to their voices.

It is important that they should communicate their views as effectively and to as many people as possible. It is equally important, therefore, that a theatre like the Royal Court, because of its close contacts with many writers and its history of breaking new ground in methods and styles of production, is both committed and involved. It was agreed at the outset, however, that any professional skills the theatre could offer were not to be used to interfere with what the company wanted to say — with content — but to heighten the group's clarity and impact in saying it.

Restraint in professional leadership is essential and not everyone is ideal for this work. The professionals have to respond to the group, and not the other way round. But we hoped that over a period of time, this interaction would affect the professionals' perspectives on their own working processes and have some impact on the Court as a whole both artistically and socially.

In approaching the work itself we try to keep in mind some of the special qualities of the companies: a capacity for a great deal of fun and enjoyment; raw energy; naturalness; a high level of imagination and intuition coupled with a real desire to learn.

Our aims with the Activists are both social and artistic. These cannot be separated in practice. It would not be enough to produce a brilliant play if the company neither cared for nor understood it; nor would it be enough to have a remarkable group experience which resulted in a piece of theatre that nobody but the performers understood or wanted to watch. We are in the business of producing good theatre and artistic aims therefore have a high priority. But we are working with young people who, although they have a great deal to say in the theatre, are often, to begin with, insecure and confused in saying it.

GETTING ORGANIZED

The group decided quite early on that productions would normally demand about three nights a week and most weekends. This is a heavy commitment and alternative activities taking up one session a week are made available, including writers's workshops, lectures and practical sessions. Fees have to be low if we are to be really accessible. At the time of writing the cost is £4 a year for the employed and £2 for the unemployed and those at school. The age limit was set at 16–23. This proves to be flexible but there are problems in having too wide an age range in a single company.

Little publicity was needed to get the group underway. We used the programmes of the theatre together with local papers and magazines. Word of mouth quickly became the normal method of recruitment. The company soon started its own magazine, later to become a monthly news-sheet, and a regular newsletter was sent out to the whole membership which stabilized eventually at about two hundred with an average of fifty involved in any one season.

IN PRACTICE

The following three examples of work with the Activists illustrate some of the unique opportunities and problems in this work.

The starting point for the Activists' Christmas 1977 project, *The Essence of Being Clean*, was the failure of a commissioned play to appear on time. With only ten weeks to prepare a major production, I approached the then resident playwright at the Royal Court, Nigel Baldwin, and decided that, given a head start, a production could be mounted. This meant deciding in advance on a theme for the show and taking a firm control over the ways in which the company would explore it. We settled on two themes which, as individuals we found compelling: political internment and commercial exploitation of the need, especially among young people, to belong to a cult or movement. These were the starting points when we met the company. For five weeks, three nights a week and at weekends, we worked with them exploring and researching these themes through discussion and improvisation.

During the day the two of us would talk about the group's work and ideas of the night before, and discuss the gradually emerging play. Nigel Baldwin would spend the rest of the day producing short scenes or monologues or just a series of lines to provide the basis of the next session with the company. We were therefore making many planning and artistic decisions on their behalf which we felt was necessary in the circumstances but unfortunate in principle, although the company was involved throughout in developing the material and colouring it with their own experience and attitudes. We spent the five weeks following the reading of the draft script rewriting with the group, clarifying the attitudes and ideas of the play, and testing how effectively they were being communicated. From the first meeting we had emphasized the need for clarity both in discussion and in physical work and the need for physical fitness and discipline. We organized strenuous half-hour warm-ups before each session so that the company got used to joining in immediately. This paid dividends for everybody once the rehearsal process began in earnest. A major problem when time is short is creating the necessary atmosphere of timelessness for the important discussions. In some ways lack of time can help all of us by forcing efficiency and professionalism in the work. But often the company would feel that important discussions were taking too long, 'so let's get on with it quick'. This is dangerous. The consequences of hasty decisions tend to mature when it's too late to do anything about them. Towards the end of the research period some of our discussions were becoming so time conscious that they were often, ironically, an actual waste of time.

To resolve this we took the group away from London for a residential working weekend. They worked, ate and slept in the same three rooms. Immediately there were no distractions during rehearsals, there was equal status within the group and a timeless quality to the discussions – no late buses to catch or irate parents to return to. The members of the group became closer to each other and the work became more sensitive. It heightened a normally bleak period of the process. The concentration level went up – and they all had a great time!

An important aspect of such a project is the relationship between the writer and director. Although good personal friends, our professional roles during this project fluctuated and occasionally jarred. In the early stages, the writer needed constant feeding either from me or from the group. As he built up a picture of the play, however, things began to change. His vision of the play became clear and immediate and he would then share the leading of the sessions. The company responded very positively to these different approaches and found the rare willingness of the writer to hand the script over to them extremely rewarding.

One of the specific aims of this project was to convince the staff of the Royal Court of the value of the theatre being used for this sort of work. There were those who had little time for the club and rankled at the idea of the Theatre Upstairs being used for an amateur production. There had already been occasional murmurings of, 'too many school parties' and, 'I never got all this fuss when I was their age'. There were others who felt there were enough problems in 'getting a pro show on without this lot traipsing about'. Critics were in a minority but the company was determined to demonstrate the value of what they were doing. The staff were invited to come and watch what was going on and their professional advice was asked. Most theatre staff have good reason to be union conscious and doing something for nothing, even if they want to, is a dangerous and exploitable precedent to set. This production had barely enough money and it was only when one technical head of department agreed to help that the other staff offered their encouragement and expertise.

Funding is always difficult and anomalous. The Arts Council of Great Britain paid the writer's commission fee but it could not support the production because it was by young amateurs. Theoretically the Youth Service could only pay for work done by youngsters in their local area whereas the Regional Arts Association could only contribute if the production toured Greater London. We eventually raised part of the money by a time-consuming assault on local and national industry: turning down one offer which was conditional on a right to alter the content of the show.

Although in many ways we were pleased with the show, we were very concerned about the extent to which we were really responding to the company's needs. Several small projects had come from individuals but to make them worthwhile involved a lot of individual attention. Inevitably, there was competition about whose idea was going to be done next. In the Festival of Summer 1978, we set out to cope with these problems.

Our aim was to give a larger company complete control over the planning and production of a week's activities for young people in the local area. With a large professional staff and a reasonable budget we hoped to provide an umbrella for many projects and to help members of the company, who had been unable to give up all their spare time for previous projects, to contribute creatively to the Festival. Politically we wanted to develop the essential links between the Youth Service and the Company to our mutual benefit. The Youth Service had agreed to finance the Festival and this was an important step in establishing the value of the service we were offering the community. By asking a group of young people to produce a

Festival for other young people we were, in effect, doubling the facility.

Forty-six members signed up to take part and after two meetings they were formed into four groups according to the amount of time they had available. The responsibility for organizing and running the Festival was spread across the groups with members sitting on publicity, design, stage-management and bookings committees. We were right in anticipating that if we created a vacuum the ideas would begin to pour in. But, as always, there was the need to listen to each other's thoughts and evaluate them carefully throughout the initial period of work. We had given the company a lot of power over decision-making and any manipulation by the staff would have broken trust and respect. The six staff who worked as members of the groups were on hand for their experience rather than as prime-movers. The Festival week itself finally comprised a new play, *Metropolitan*, about attitudes to life in London, a number of satirical cabarets, a series of shadow puppet plays, various shows by visiting youth theatre groups, an exhibition of members' pottery and musical combinations in the company. To our astonishment the company decided against doing a play for young children. They felt that there was too little money to go round and it was better to do less, and do it well. This was fine, but it put us in a difficult position with the Youth Service.

We had to put in an application for a Festival grant before the company began work so many of our proposals were vague. Nevertheless they had included running a play for younger children as this had originally been a popular idea among the company. When the grant was lower than expected they dropped the idea. The resulting confusion was enormous and underlined the need for both the Youth Service and the Youth Theatre better to understand each other's processes of work. Youth Theatre has to find people within bureaucracies to help it and then go out of its way to help them. Only then will this interaction pay off.

The Festival made particular demands on the staff. They could never see their work as just a job, because the group demanded far more than just a formal commitment. It is essential to hold back some professional expertise, to resist the temptation to hurry the process along, and to accept the pressure and insecurity of not being sure of what is going to happen. All the groups pushed the negotiation period of the work to the limit leaving very little time for rehearsal. But during this final period they recognized the need for a disciplined director/actor relationship and deliberately handed back power to the professionals.

For the Christmas 1978 show, *Blame it on the Boogie*, we turned again to the production of a full-length play. The commissioned writer, Gilly Fraser, wanted to explore themes to do with relationships, particularly sexual, among young people. Two directors, a designer, and the recently appointed full-time youth worker made up the rest of the staff. There was a schedule of six weeks' research and six weeks' rehearsal. This was a difficult subject to tackle with such a cross-section of ages in the group and different levels of maturity. We wanted to let the group control the degree to which they made their personal feelings public. We began by playing a series of games which involved everybody talking about themselves. We then asked for individuals to relate particular events in their own lives and to direct other members of the company in enacting them. Everyone was encouraged to contribute their ideas and feelings in writing, anonymously if they wanted, to a pool of material for the writer.

The degree of honesty increased as we began to look more carefully at our own attitudes, although we had constantly to remind ourselves of the dangers of becoming voyeurs of each other's problems, a danger the group understood and were quick to point out if the questioning became too personal. Most of us, including the staff, felt ignorant or foolish at one time or another and this generated a quick sense of learning together. Nevertheless, the theme of the production did create tensions within the group which couldn't be ignored. To allay outside doubts we held an open night for parents and others to come and watch the company at work, and the few who attended, including some of the theatre staff, were strongly committed to the production at the end of the evening. The personalities of the individual staff can have a considerable effect on a Youth Theatre and on the work it produces by affecting so much the atmosphere in which ideas are offered and used. The participation of the youth worker became increasingly important during the production in helping to objectify the processes we were going through and in being available to the group in a different capacity from the directors.

The writer was faced with a difficult task in this production.

She felt set apart from the staff and the company to begin with, coming from a predominantly television background and being older than the rest. She approached the work at first as a professional doing a job and was very concerned about how we expected the play to be written. She didn't want to interfere with her normal process of playwriting. As the work progressed, however, and she saw the group working on and developing ideas she suggested, the barriers began to break down and she began to find great enjoyment in the work. Partly to raise funds we organized a sponsored day-long conference around a performance and the company involved themselves in discussing the theme 'Talking About Sex' with social workers, teachers and sexologists. The Royal Court allowed the company an unheard of one-week to set up in the Theatre Upstairs and a two-week run which was extended after Christmas after selling out. The subsequent reviews in the national press and the evident support of the theatre suggest that the voices of one group of young people had, for a period of time, been given 'power and status'.

We are still questioning and re-assessing our Youth Theatre work at the Royal Court. Of some things, however, we are sure. We must maintain our open door and spread our activities to include as many people as possible. The qualifications must stay the same: time and the desire to communicate. We must take care to encourage professionals to get involved who understand that they have, in their skills, a great deal to offer, but that they must not dominate. And we must review our priorities for next time in the light of each project. Youth Theatre is now a growing industry. It has to be carefully thought about if it is not to become another inward-looking elitism, remote from and of no interest to, the majority of young people.

Conclusions

Looking in general at the work which John Dale and I have done at the Y.P.T.S., I think it is useful to isolate certain crucial issues for the development of Young People's Theatre. Most important is the cultural 'apartheid' that discriminates different types of art for different types of people. These divisions are fundamentally class ones, based on earning capacity and the amount of power we have in controlling our financial security. Part of the process of education (some would say it was the whole process) is to prepare children for the labour market, but the great challenge is that until they become wage-earners children are in some respects classless. Theatre can offer the most adventurous aspects of modern drama in an attempt to influence children's thinking and thereby strive to change society, as indeed many teachers are doing. This does not happen very much of course, because children can very easily inherit bourgeois values not just from home and school but also from what little theatre they are allowed to see. As a recent report points out: 'Children, and to a lesser extent teenagers, do not go to the theatre on their own. They experience theatre as part of their community culture, or organized for them by adults, whether in the school hall or at the end of a coach trip.'[26]

So a lot depends on the structures which exist, in school, in a theatre, in a local education authority, in society itself, to make theatre available to children. This means a deeply thought-out approach to the problem instead of an attitude that merely sees children as easy audience fodder. Schools' matinees are assiduously organized, or special plays for children performed at Christmas time. Most managements budget children's plays more cheaply because the ticket prices are likely to be lower. A favourite alternative is to mount productions of examination set texts. The I.L.E.A. even goes as far as publishing the exact numbers of children studying a particular play[27] and sending them to theatres so as to help fulfil the financial administrator's dream of predicting exact box office returns! These solutions are at best stop-gaps and at worst patronizing because they treat children as a special category; not as people in their own right, but as immature adults to be trained as an audience for the future, or as a sociological statistic, an examination class.

Children are treated as second-class citizens because they have little economic and no political power, and the art that is provided for them usually reflects their status: it is literally as well as culturally poverty-stricken. The provision of formal education seems also to have exacerbated class divisions and made it harder, not easier, for working-class children to get other than working-class jobs.[28] The prospect of unemployment for a huge proportion of school leavers is now accepted as a permanent state of affairs. To solve this the euphemism 'leisure society' has been coined to hold out a kind of consolation prize for those who are trapped by the shrinking labour market, or have been refused entry into the middle-class meritocracy despite their academic abilities (a common enough plight for young blacks). Community workers and youth leaders have been looking to the Arts as a means of coping with 'the deprived' who otherwise find themselves idle on the streets and prone to increasing harassment under the notorious 'Sus' laws.[29] The Youth Service itself is chronically underfinanced as well as largely ignorant of the nature of the professional Arts: the result is often mere papering over the cracks, a misuse of energy and a misuse of artistic potential.[30]

The emphasis on humanities lessons at school must ultimately confront freedom of creative expression with the unfreedoms of the labour process. For many young people the solution to this dilemma is either adopting the culture of the outlaw which vandalizes an already alien environment, or the culture of self-oppression which anticipates a future failure early enough to make it an acceptable way of life. The strain of despair found in young people's writing coupled with the alarmingly high (and unprecedented) incidence of teenage alcoholism and suicide are vivid examples of this. Many black youths, more acutely aware than their white peers of the unfreedoms of leaving school and therefore of the hypocrisy of teachers' claims, deliberately under-achieve because they want to *prove* that their teachers will have failed them in the long run. Far from humanizing, the humanities seem to tyrannize. For many, therefore, Art can come to mean powerlessness, a code of 'mucking about', first learnt at school and then carried on into working life. Drama may be a 'soft' option, often only patronizingly available to remedial or non-academic children in the school's curriculum. A trip to the theatre becomes simply a way of avoiding school, and either the theatre goes out of its way to indicate that the school visit is 'special', 'not routine' or just a 'plain bloody nuisance', or it seats them all next to a clearly middle-class audience who 'behave' and who also seem to be enjoying a soft option in life.[31] The few theatres that try to break down this elitism not only have to cope with children's own inheritance of bourgeois values, but also with the pathetic scraps of subsidy thrown at them from off the table of the Arts Council's richest clients.

Meanwhile, Army posters appeal more effectively than do

'socio-cultural animateurs' (as community artists are now calling themselves) to the fantasies of an enervated youth population. 'Mucking about' is no longer a symptom of powerlessness if it means having a real gun in your hand. One lad who volunteered to be a mercenary in Zaire came up with a startling new version of the children's fantasy about living for ever: 'I believe there is life after death. I know it. Anybody who says there isn't, I'll smash his face in.'[32]

These paradoxes are at the heart of a divided society: they are clearly analysed in a play like *Spring Awakening* where, like a gruesome epilogue, the play's survivors grow up merely to be slaughtered in the trenches of the First World War.[33]

Just as racial apartheid depends on people's collusion with the idea that blacks are not just inferior but, *sui generis*, different from whites, cultural apartheid depends on colluding with an illusory model of society. This model separates the artist from the rest of society, imbuing him or her with special privileges or even mystical powers. Eccentric, refined, kept apart from others, the professional artist becomes a different sort of human being. Artists have often been called 'children' and indeed both are often denied real influence, sharing the patronizing suspicion of a so-called responsible society.

Yet despite this denial of a common and shared humanity towards artists and children, the received notion of what is civilized and to be treasured as central to our humanity is not a board meeting or trades union strike, but a great play or opera. Great benefactors like Rockefeller prove the point by clearing the slum housing of thousands of families so as to build a shiny new Arts Centre (which those families will never enter, at least not at New York ticket prices). Thus the forces of privilege have lain waste working class neighbourhoods in the name of some fraudulent notion of Art which in effect veils the ostentatious exclusivity of their elitist practices. Where is the philanthropy in that?[34]

The Arts bear a fearful responsibility for they can collude with all the other major forces that distort reality. The art we teach children for free at school is snatched away from them, packaged and sold back at an impossible social price. It is right that children should eschew it.

Drama cannot help but dirty its hands; it is rooted in the prevailing myths or the actual truth about society; it proves what it believes in, whether it likes it or not. Like teaching, Art attempts to make sense or nonsense of the world and children respond more immediately than adults to this sense or nonsense because they have less to lose. Most children avoid the theatre because it makes nonsense; some, who are not cowed by them, also truant from their schools for the same reasons. The functions of theatre and of education, therefore must be to make sense of the world, and thereby commit us to changing it to a better, more egalitarian world as well. Like litmus paper, the child's response measures, more effectively than anyone else's, the complexion of honesty which Art or Education bear in relation to society.

There is no special kind of art reserved for children; it all belongs to them as of right, the classics along with the best and most adventurous in modern drama, the great performances by the greatest actors along with the youth theatre plays devised by children themselves. As they grow up, they are learning to be human and this means having a creative engagement with life. Creativity, as we have seen, encounters many blocks to its fulfilment: it is continually tested against reality. Because children are not so easily misled by old solutions to familiar problems, their creativity can become a logical and exacting exploration of human (or dehumanized) society. It can also be quickly destroyed (and at an early age) by their parental culture precisely because they inherit their parents' society. However, the change towards an integrated society can only begin with a culture shared by adults *and* children, a culture that is lived, not fantasized, a culture that finds theatre in life, that is indeed 'real' and not just 'theatrical'.

Cultural

Apartheid.

6. Drama, Theatre and Social Reality

Ken Robinson

There has been a determination in recent years to strengthen the position of drama in the school curriculum by clarifying just what it is that this work contributes to children's development. I want to argue here that the past emphasis on 'creativity', 'self-expression' and 'individuality' has helped to divert attention from some of the most important functions of drama in schools. Far from furthering progressive hopes in education, these ideas have sometimes led to forms of teaching, in all subjects in schools, which have reinforced quite reactionary values. Instead of helping children to express themselves and think clearly, some forms of 'creative self-expression' may have been having just the opposite effect. Children's own work in the arts needs to be related to an understanding of realized art forms: or, in this case, their own expressive work through drama should include watching and taking part in theatre activities and understanding something of written plays. This is not because the touch of an old master is good for you, aesthetically speaking, but because the main value of drama, as I see it, is as a form of social edu-cation, and educational drama and theatre share some of the same social functions.

The division between drama and theatre which the Riverside Conference and this book set out to discuss has opened up quite recently. It is not a natural law. It is helpful, I think, to reflect briefly on how it came about in the first place.

The use of drama in schools goes back as far as schooling itself. It is by no means a bright-eyed newcomer. But 'drama' in an educational setting has not always meant the same thing nor has it always been taught in the same way. In its earliest forms, drama in schools meant play-acting. In fact the deepest roots of the theatre in this country are tangled up in those of school drama. In the pre- and early Elizabethan period, before the emergence of a separate professional class in the theatre, 'The school-boys were simply one of the many independent groups of drama producers. The plays they acted were as much a part of the English drama of their day as any other plays in the kingdom.'[1]

The rise of the professional companies, dating roughly from the foundation, in London, of The Theatre in 1576, slowly edged the non-professional companies, including the school-boys, away from the centre of theatrical innovation. From the early days of the Restoration the influence of the school drama declined as the young companies withdrew into performances within and for the schools themselves. It was not until the eighteenth century that interest revived in the uses of drama in schools, not this time as a source of theatrical innovation of public entertainment, but as a means of education.

For the first four hundred years or so of its development in schools, then, drama meant acting plays and learning about dramatic literature. The only difference anyone could see between the terms 'drama' and 'theatre' was that one referred to the stock of dramatic texts and the other to the business of performing it. It is in this sense that the early reports on the curriculum of this century wholeheartedly endorsed the value of dramatic activity in schools. The educational results were plain to see: 'The pupils who take part in performance of plays learn to speak well and to express emotion becomingly; to be expressive yet restrained; to subordinate the individual to the whole; to play the game; to be resourceful and self possessed and mitigate personal disabilities'[2]

Thus spake the Board of Education in 1919, adding trenchantly, 'It will hardly be suggested that these are negligible accomplishments.'[3] In the years between the wars, the influence of drama slowly spread through the school system until in 1938 a new book appeared which could triumphantly report on 'the final vindication of drama in schools'.[4] The authors of The School Drama estimated that the numbers of schools both elementary, and secondary 'where acting has now become a normal feature of school life, must now run into thousands.'[5] For it was now no secret, they revealed, that the value of drama 'as a cultural exercise, is now almost universally admitted and that the H.M. Board of Education has given its official sanction and blessing to the good work'.[6]

Outside the schools, the 1930s had seen a tidal wave of amateur theatre groups which continued to swell after the war until, in 1952 for example, there were reckoned to be about 30,000[7] such companies up and down the country. Generally speaking drama in schools during the 1930s and 1940s had come to mean two things: training in speech and practical work on plays – acting. The purpose of this was both to encourage self-expression and to provide a 'rudimentary dramatic training . . . in the belief that the exercise of such a training has a benefit all of its own'.[8] There was a vigorous professional organization on the move, the Association of Teachers of Speech and Drama, and this was running regular conferences and courses on topics from 'Production in Little Theatres' to 'The Psychology of the Development of Speech'.[9]

Drama in schools was still a pretty formal business. *The School Drama* recommended that fair notice be given of all 'acting lessons' and that a strict procedure be adopted. Where space was available a standard size stage should be marked out on the floor with tapes and all preparations should be under the charge of a stage-manager, chosen from the class, who could be changed from month to month and should take directions from the producer of the moment.

One of the reasons why drama took such a grip during this time was that there was a shift in the educational climate as a whole. The developing field of child psychology, for example, was beginning to give a new prominence to the value of play and 'learning through experience'. Indeed the Hadow Report on the primary school curriculum had pronounced that the work there should be thought of in terms of 'activity and experience rather than of knowledge to be acquired and facts to be stored'.[10] The feeling was that, if the psychologists were right, the key to education was 'the experience, curiosity and the awakening powers and interest of the children themselves'.[11]

Self-expression and creativity were now coming by many to be seen as the real point of drama in schools. This view was not without its critics. One of them, developing a theme which was not to abate in the years to come, argued that 'acting should be done out of school time . . . and should be recognized as an important part of education for it taught how to express personality, so much more valuable than the much lauded self-expression'. Speaking of acting classics, the boys should learn 'to stand well, move well and speak the verse well. Shakespeare could be relied on to do the rest and boys had learnt something worth learning.'[12]

Self-expression was not without its supporters either. When, after the war, teachers set about working the Education Act of 1944, a revised idea of what drama was began to take root and it was this view which eventually drove a wedge between drama and theatre activities in many schools.

THE BIRTH OF CHILD DRAMA

In 1943 a group of teachers met in Birmingham to form the Educational Drama Association, 'to foster an interest in drama in schools'. Four years later Peter Slade was appointed as Drama Adviser for Birmingham and became Chairman of the E.D.A. He opened the Experimental Drama Centre in Rea Street and began to develop a view of drama based on many years of work with children and adults. He published his views in 1954, in *Child Drama*[13] edited by Brian Way, and in doing so set the teaching of drama on a new course, away from theatre.

It was Slade's view that, what he called, Child Drama was an art form in its own right, quite distinct from theatre as understood by adults. It grows from a natural source within children and the teacher's task is simply to provide the right conditions for this to happen. Drama is not a subject, or a method of teaching, 'It is the great activity, it never ceases where there is life; it is eternally bound up with mental health. It is the Art of Living.'[14] The teacher's job is not to teach skills and techniques of performance, but to nurture this tender art. To do this, the teacher must learn to relate to the children in a new role: that of a 'loving ally'.[15] Only two qualities need to be fostered: *absorption* and *sincerity*.

Child Drama, he argued, has its roots in play. It is part of the innocence and sanctity of childhood.[16] Its purpose is to develop the child from within through creative self-expression. Peter Slade was not alone in wanting to do this. Many books which came after *Child Drama* put the same view. Neither was he the first to see the potential of play in education. His influence was as strong as it was, when it was, because like many innovators, he expressed a prevailing mood. He did not invent a whole new set of educational priorities. He put into articulate form the kind of values which many of his contemporaries were feeling intuitively to be right. He showed that drama was a natural way to achieve the kind of objectives in schools which were coming to be seen as of paramount importance.

During the 1940s and 1950s there was a creeping unrest with the materialism which had come to dominate postwar society and its institutions, including education. The attempts of successive peace-time governments to create a land of plenty and well-being with the new technologies were having an unexpected social cost. This was not going unnoticed. One attempt to address these problems took place in 1957 at the Festival Hall, where Herbert Read spoke out on the subject of 'Humanity, Technology and Education'.[17]

> The ideal of education, is no longer the development of the whole man, much less the creation of a gentleman: it is an intensive search for special aptitudes and the development of a chosen aptitude into a particular technique. We are told that our survival as a nation depends on this partial and specialized form of education. Our civilization is no longer primarily human. Mechanization has taken command and the human being becomes a component of the machine.[18]

As he saw it, the pre-occupation with technological advance was turning schools and colleges into production lines of myopic specialists. Vocationalism in education, he said, had been invented purely to conform with specialism in industry.

> The ideal of technology is complete automation – a machine that controls itself without human intervention. The corresponding ideal of education is a human brain that controls itself free from all idealistic entanglements, free above all from originality of any kind. Functional thinking is like functional machinery: cold, precise, imageless, repetitive, bloodless, nerveless, dead.[19]

The idea that society is plotting its own brain death, that human relations are becoming increasingly impoverished and the creative spirit emaciated, provide fertile conditions for the reception of the principles of Child Drama with its call for a return to individuality and re-affirmation of the warm purity of childhood.

The vigour with which the ideas of 'child-centred education', creativity and self-expression were taken up in all areas of the

curriculum in the years to come suggests that these ideals were
not confined to the Rea Street Centre or the Festival Hall. The
time was right for Slade to point drama into the prevailing wind.
It was time for the teacher/producer with his rolls of tape and
French's Acting Edition, to give way to the loving ally and his
absorbed sincerity.

The achievement of Slade and his followers was to establish
that drama is not an isolated phenomenon of adult culture and to
challenge the accepted idea that learning to act and move well
did in fact have 'a benefit all of its own'.

In doing this he pushed drama into the mainstream of progressive education and strengthened its ideological framework
with the concepts of child psychology and liberal philosophy.
But in making these connections he helped to break off others,
and opened divisions which later writers were obliged to support
or deny.

The new conception of the role of drama in schools was by no
means confined to Britain. Parallel developments were underway in the United States – in creative dramatics – and in Canada
and in Europe. In an international survey conducted for the
International Theatre Institute of UNESCO in the early 1950s
information on drama in schools was sought in twenty-seven
countries. Eighteen of these indicated some sort of involvement
in drama in education. In introducing a paper on this survey in
1955, John Allen had this to say:

> Is [this] a new art? a new aspect of art? a new educational technique?
> We do not know. . . . But is its clear that in many countries of the
> world, educational drama represents, or shall we say, is the out-
> come of, an altogether new approach both to Education and the
> Dramatic Arts. We are engaged in fact in applying the work of
> Froebel, Dewey and Pestalozzi to the drama and that of
> Stanislavsky, Copeau and Granville-Barker to education.[20]

The value of drama activities for the growing child was
becoming less and less a matter of dispute. What was disputed
and has been ever since is how these activities connect with
theatre. Some of the key figures in the development of educational drama never insisted on the distinction in the first place.
Esmé Church, at the Young Vic, Elsie Fogerty at the Central
School of Speech and Drama, Rose Bruford, Maisie Cobby, E. J.
Burton at Trent Park, John Hodgson at Bretton Hall, and many

others saw the closest connections between theatre and education. But what sort of connection is it? Clearly actors on a stage
are doing something different from children in a drama lesson.
But do children grow up into theatre eventually? John Allen, as
Her Majesty's Inspector for Schools with national responsibility
for drama, was the author of the first official survey of the work
by the Department of Education and Science.[21]

Looking back over ten years of change in drama teaching, he
wrote in 1968, that the quantity of drama seemed to be far out-
stripping quality. He wondered whether the enormous diversity
of work which was currently going on in the name of creative
self-expression was all of equal value for children. 'Is there,' he
asked 'in the middle of this range of artistic expression a
discipline that can be identified as drama?'[22] He warned,

> . . . that the recent emphasis on improvised drama will detract from
> the importance of studying plays. Although this emphasis is partly at
> least to be explained as an escape from the literary domination of
> drama, the price that is being paid is the linguistic impoverishment of
> improvised drama. We are in grave danger of creating a situation
> where a play is something educationally offensive and the study of a
> text an undesirable activity except for a lot of eggheads.[23]

If we admit that the activities which the report described as
drama have any educational significance, he asked, 'can we deny
that they are also the beginning of a process that ends in
Shakespeare, Aeschylus and Ibsen?'[24] David Clegg, writing in
Theatre Quarterly in 1973 joined with John Allen in attacking
what he saw as sentimental and nebulous chatter about the value
of drama. Still Clegg could not accept that John Allen himself
was on the right track. Indeed he found it hard to credit, 'that
such a simple view of drama in education still retains any
currency at all.'[25]

Dorothy Heathcote and Gavin Bolton have both discussed the
connections between drama and theatre in terms of *form* in the
work and the overlap between the role of the teacher and the
playwright and director in structuring and controlling the
process. There are such formal relationships. But does this mean
then that children should actually study plays and act in them?
Should they be encouraged to go and see them? These questions
are particularly pertinent just now with the increasing involvement, through Theatre in Education and Children's Theatre, of

actors and actor/teachers in education. And after all the teacher in school is faced, not with three or four drama sessions with a group, as at Riverside but with three or four years of work with the children. During this time is it part of the job to introduce children to theatre, in addition to enabling their own expressive work to take place?

DRAMA AND THEATRE

When theatre activities were uncoupled from drama in education in the 1950s and 1960s, it was not, as we have seen, simply to lighten the load on the teacher. It was part of an accelerating change of direction which ran through arts education as a whole. The direction was straighforward enough. It was towards drawing out what was within the child – that is, its 'potential' – and to avoid stifling natural vitality and curiosity with forms of teaching which dwelt on information and formal skills. Taking part in, or learning about, the theatre was really suspect on two accounts. First because it did imply learning 'skills'. 'Spontaneity' however, had been argued to be the very pulse of self-expression, and this was easily retarded, if not arrested altogether by lingering over technique. Moreover, skills were only useful for putting things across to an audience. But now in drama there was no audience. Everyone was involved simultaneously and the product *was* the process.

Second, where the emphasis is on educating children from the inside out, teaching about realized arts forms – which other people have created – such as plays, could easily be seen as a sort of cultural imposition. And that is just how it was seen by some.

Although for many teachers the distinction between drama and theatre began as an attempt to balance the values of personal expressive work with appreciation of realized art, the result in many cases was a complete reversal of priorities in art education. Small distinctions have a habit of growing up into big dichotomies and the cost of raising this one has sometimes been high. For every teacher who felt that self-expression was an educational panacea there has been a critic to make accusations about replacing educational discipline with chaos and structured learning with disorganized bouts of primal mumbling. In the heat of the day, forthright claims about releasing vast untapped resources of creative energy have been met with despairing cries about abandoning the 'cultural heritage'.

But are these dichotomies really as genuine as our enthusiasm for them has sometimes been? Does self-expression naturally lead to self-fulfilment and does appreciation of realized art really cramp personal creativity? Does theatre get in the way of drama or vice versa?

In some senses 'drama' and 'theatre' refer to totally different things and we won't get very far in making comparisons. If we compare, for example, drama teaching as a profession with working in the theatre we can expect to find little to say so far as conditions of work and so on are concerned. Even if we compare what goes on in drama lessons to what happens inside theatres, the differences may still outweigh all other considerations *depending on what we compare*. In talking about the relationship of theatre and drama, in an educational context, it is important at the outset to be clear about what we have in mind.

By 'drama' we generally mean situations in which there is some element of tension. We use it in two ways: first, to mean actual situations in real life and second, to mean a particular type of make-believe. In educational drama and in the theatre it is used in this second sense. In the report of the Schools Council Drama Project,[26] we called the essential activity of drama in the classroom, 'acting-out'. This is a familiar enough term. We chose to use it instead of *acting* because we wanted to imply a difference in function between the activity of children or adults in the classroom or workshop and the activity of the actor on the stage. Indeed the main point I want to develop here is that drama and theatre are directly connected through these central activities – acting-out and acting – but that they do have different functions both inside and outside schools. Although acting-out is the essential feature of drama in the classroom, it is not what drama is, nor is the point of educational drama simply to get children acting-out. The *drama* is the *encounter* between those who are taking part: the events, and the tension which threads through them. Acting-out is purely the process by which drama is produced. Drama in the classroom is mostly improvised, and has no *separate* audience.

'Theatre' also means a type of social encounter: one centred on a performance and with a separate audience. 'Theatre' does not refer to what the actors do nor to the presence of the audience. It refers to the encounter which takes place between them. Take away half of this and you will be left with nothing we could call theatre. Drama and theatre are not separate but they are different.

The audience do not watch theatre: they watch a drama. They *participate* in theatre because it is partly their presence and their activity which identifies what is going on as theatre. This raises two further points. First, this does not mean that the difference between drama and theatre is simply that one has an audience and the other does not or even that everyone is actively involved if it is drama and half the room is passive if it is theatre.

As I will argue later, the participants in a drama lesson work with a *sense of audience* whether or not there is actually a separate group of people looking on. Moreover, the audience in a theatre is not passive. They are as actively involved as the actors, at least potentially. Without their active involvement there is no communication and there is therefore no theatre. This question of communication in the arts will also need to be considered later.

Second, the mere fact that an event has an audience does not mean that it is therefore theatre. The work at the Riverside Studios illustrated this quite clearly. Although there was an audience at each of the sessions we would not call what was going on there, theatre. The difference is in the sense of convention and sense of intention of those who were taking part. The audience knew that they were watching improvised exploratory work and understood that, although the children and actors were working with a sense of audience, they were not for the most part aiming to communicate directly *to* the audience. The exceptions were in Bill Gaskill's sessions whenever he asked the actors to work for the audience. He thereby changed what was going on from improvised drama to improvised theatre. There is no theatre without the intention to communicate and the attention of an active audience.

In comparing drama and theatre then, I am comparing two types of social encounter which use elements of make-believe and forms of role-play. I am not comparing the professional superstructures which have grown up around them.

DISPOSABLE DRAMA

We can't begin to make sense of drama or theatre if we approach them as isolated phenomena, unconnected with anything else we do. Neither drama nor theatre have been invented by anyone. Harold Rosen once said that drama is as cheap as dirt. He meant that the raw materials of drama and theatre are among the most common elements in human behaviour and social action. We have a fundamental capacity for dramatizing which is as common as language and gesture: the capacity to represent; to let one action or experience stand for or mean another. It begins early in childhood as symbolic play and it persists into maturity and beyond in the capacity to take on a role. There is nothing unusual in this. One of the most common techniques of every-day conversation is to slip into a role to make a point or describe an event or to depict someone we know. We take on the personalities of others to bring them to life for the listener and *to add our own commentary on them through the way we represent them.*

It may be a large jump from this easy facility to the sophisti-cated artistry of the professional actor but the basic capacity is the same. We dramatize all the time whether teachers ask us to or not, with or without a grant from the Arts Council.

Drama teachers and those in the theatre have not invented this capacity, any more than a sculptor invents the stone he works with. They use it to some specific purpose.

In most cases in everyday life our dramatizing is disposable. That is we take on a quick role to make a point, to entertain, inform, persuade. Our use of role is informal, casual and has an immediate purpose. The make-believe world we create for that moment and that purpose may not be used again.

The dramatist also creates a world of make-believe. But in doing so takes great care, as Nicholas Wright has described, to control its form and structure. Our response to a play is not just to the various events which it portrays as they unfold one by one, but to the play as a whole when its performance is complete. The meaning of the play is partly contained in the way it represents its world and not simply in what it represents. The drama is formed in a certain way and not in another and this is crucial for its effect. It is not disposable. The difference in these two examples of dramatizing is really one of formality and intention.

Somewhere between these two extremes we can locate the type of work that goes on in educational drama sessions and also the improvisational techniques of rehearsals and so on. Very often the drama which is created and used in teaching is dispo-sable. It was in Gavin Bolton's and Dorothy Heathcote's sessions at Riverside and in Bill Gaskill's work. I mean they were not trying to create a drama to be refined and worked on again and again. Dorothy and Gavin wanted to use the children's capacity for dramatizing to help them explore some specific ideas and feelings. Similarly Bill Gaskill was using drama to investigate certain events. [The function of the drama in all of these cases was explorative. But it has other functions and markedly so when we consider its use in theatre. As the function changes, so the drama itself may become more or less arresting in itself, more or less disposable.]

People have not been slow to recognize that children dramatize almost from the moment they open their eyes. But if they do it all of the time, why make them do it in school? I once heard someone say, 'We don't make children do drama in school. We allow them to do it.' I think that anyone who has spent any time trying to 'allow' an unwilling fourth form to do drama will find this curious. I want to come back later to why it should be, if it is so natural, that so many children genuinely find it difficult to get involved in drama work. But I want to look first at two of the reasons why it has often been said in the past that they should do it: first, because it encourages self-expression and second, because this in turn develops the individual. These ideas have probably done more than anything else in their time to obscure the most important characteristics and functions of drama in schools and in doing so to disguise its connections with theatre.

CHAOS, ANARCHY AND SELF-EXPRESSION

In much that has been written about drama in schools there is a tendency to treat it as a kind of chemical additive. [So, we hear that, 'drama' develops the whole person; or, 'drama' makes children more sensitive. Alternatively drama is personified. It then seems to work educational changes all of its own accord, independently of what the teacher gets up to.] For example: 'Drama not only helps the child to control himself for his own benefit but what is more important helps him to control his own reaction when he needs to be with or work with other people.'[27] The danger in talking about drama as some kind of independent force like this is that we can end up thinking that in drama teaching we are simply stimulating a natural process of self-development in children, which tracks the same course once it's under way no matter what the teacher does.

We can be led to feel that our own values and attitudes hardly come into it. This can lead to some startling contradictions particularly when the talk turns to developing children's 'individuality'. Consider the following quotations.

[In drama] . . . the individual has to make decisions about morals. By making situations conscious, the child is able to look at life as an observer and make slow inward decisions. It is greatly to the credit of Young People that when they have to face *truth* in this way, as long as they are unhurried, they nearly always choose *the right set of values* and behave accordingly.[28] (My italics.)

In encouraging truth and sincerity, the teacher must be prepared for the results to be occasionally unpalatable: they must be accepted as valid creative work although it should not in any way be suggested that the attitudes to life shown are condoned. Nevertheless opportunities must be given for playing-out crude notions of life. To ignore or suppress them is to suggest that some creative activities are forbidden by adults.[29]

Both of these were written some time ago and the authors would probably want to qualify them now. I quote them because, in a rare way, they make explicit some of the unspoken hopes which have been held out for self-expression.

The idea seems to have been that self-expression and creativity are just naturally good things. *What* is expressed and created may not be, but the end justifies the means because the child is subsequently transformed into a responsible individual, like base metal into gold, by this alchemical process of expressing him/herself. This works by purging psychic impurities which are 'played-out'. The dilemma of letting the children express unacceptable ideas is only temporary because in the process they will discharge these unpalatable attitudes without the teacher having to arbitrate in matters of good taste.

It is worth asking why it should be, if the end of this process is so predictable, that those who speak of allowing individuality to just develop generally go on to specify exactly what sort of individual they have in mind. [Usually they are hoping for someone who is sensitive, aware, confident, imaginative, well-adjusted to society and so on: children who come to see 'the right set of values' in the end. If we really do mean developing *individuality* perhaps we should at least stop cataloguing all of the ways in which these individuals will be more or less the same.]

[Perhaps we must also recognize that adjusting to prevailing social values and roles is not the most characteristic mark of 'an individual'. Even talking about developing 'individuality' is riddled with social values but in the past the assumption seems to have been that, given enough psychic space in which to expand freely, children will naturally develop the same attitudes as everybody else and fit in snugly.]

It is interesting that a process which has been justified in the past in such overtly conservative terms should have acquired a reputation for anarchy and subversion in some schools. There are two reasons for this. There have been many teachers who have recognized the real implications of individuality and have set about bringing them into effect. This actually is subversive. But the second, and for some considerable time, more common reason was that the practice of self-expression and creativity was really no clearer than the precept. 'Self-expression', for a time, was rather like the diplomat's bag. You could put its name on anything and get it through. Chaos only turns into anarchy when there is some deliberate point to it. I think we might as well admit that in some of the most advanced cases of self-expression, even anarchy would have been difficult to organize.

This is not really so surprising when teachers new to drama could turn at one time to official reports for guidance and read that in the drama lesson:

> The freest type of discipline is necessary if the children's powers of self-expression are to be encouraged. Directions from the teacher should therefore be as few as possible . . . so that [drama] for the children always provides a creative experience and opportunity for the free use of imagination and the exercise of self-expression.[30]

This is really the most damaging implication of the unqualified doctrine of self-expression and creativity: the idea that children arrive at self-realization by some kind of expressive homing instinct with the teacher only occasionally correcting their course by the guiding shake of a tambourine.

It is important to bury these ideas because they have continued to dominate the popular image of drama teaching despite the fact that drama teachers themselves have long since begun to move on to a more structured form of work which makes greater demands on the children and on them. Putting creative activity to some effect requires control, discipline, and skill. Drama and the other arts have an expressive function. But self-expression is not strictly speaking the point of them. The difference is an important one.

EXPRESSIVE BEHAVIOUR AND EXPRESSIVE ACTION

None of us consists of a single unique sense of self which we can casually express when called on. Personal consciousness is a maelstrom of competing self-images which shuffle and blend continuously according to past experience, immediate events and the subjective states they produce. A child or adult who is simply asked to express him/herself could be forgiven for asking, 'Which one? and for giving a different answer according to the time of day. Simply giving out energy is not necessarily expressive in any way which is educationally useful or valuable.

⌊In any act of expression it is not, strictly speaking, our 'self' that we express. What we express are the attitudes and beliefs we hold, the ideas we have and the emotions we feel which may conflict with and contradict each other. And these attitudes and beliefs, ideas and emotions – and this is the crucial point – are always *about* something: and so must drama be and so must the arts. We cannot create drama about nothing, and for what we do to be *expressive* we must feel an involvement with whatever the work is about.⌋

Not all behaviour is expressive. If I am driving a car my physical activities need not in themselves be expressing anything. They may not even be conscious. But if I am driving the car hard after an argument with someone it is quite likely that my behaviour is expressive. The difference is that when we are being expressive we are acting in accordance with a particular disposition: anger or frustration in this case.

In his clear analysis of expression, Alan Tormey,[31] talks of what he calls the intentional object of a particular mental state or attitude. He says, by way of example, that: 'If I am fascinated *by* centaurs, apprehensive *over* money, angry *with* the cook or afraid *of* the dark, the centaurs, the money, the cook and the dark are the intentional objects of these states.'[32] They are what stimulate or provoke the state which is being expressed.

⌊An expression is always both *of* and *about* something.⌋ If, for example, we see someone crying we may wonder that the crying is expressive of – hunger, grief, joy – and also what the expression is about – why are they crying? As Tormey points out, the answer to the first question is not always an answer to the second. The first question is asking for a description of what the 'intentional state' is and the second for a description of the 'intentional object' of the state. And according to Tormey, 'We can ask both questions meaningfully of any instance of expressive behaviour.'[33]

The exact failing of some so-called expressive work in schools and elsewhere is that we could not ask these two questions of it. [Getting children to 'express grief', for example, without any sense of context or impulse to do so only produces imitative behaviour which is not about anything and therefore not genuinely *of* anything either. It is not a genuine act of expression at all, because in both senses of this word, it has no *object*. It encourages children to wear the mask of expressive behaviour; to practise simply what it looks like.] The alternative to this is not necessarily to supply the children with *real* intentional objects as in a lesson I once saw, where the teacher decided to look at 'grief' because she knew that the mother of one the girls in the class had actually died. This is clearly not the answer.

[In drama we create an '*intentional context*', a world where we know the events are not real but a metaphor for real events. The quality of feeling in drama, and therefore of expression, is to do with the degree to which the group can identify with, and generate an attitude to, the issues and events which the drama represents.] There is always a sense of operating on two levels in drama which we need to come back to in more detail later. They are separated purely by a sense of convention. In Dorothy Heathcote's first session the children who complained, as pilgrims, about the Captain's insensitivity were being expressive of a feeling and a mood they experienced only within the confines of the depicted world of the drama. When she stopped to speak to them as herself, the children would not then be experiencing the same feeling because it existed only within that intentional context. The trouble with some drama work is either that the teacher, in attempts to generate self-expression, tries to stimulate only actual expressions of real feelings, or when the drama begins does not manage to generate any sense of something to be expressed at all.

There is another important distinction to be made here between *expressive* behaviour and *expressive action*. Some of my expressions are quite involuntary and others are quite deliberate. If I am stung by a wasp and flail my arms around, crying aloud, most people would guess that I was expressing something. I would be. But it would be involuntarily. But if I give someone a present out of friendship, I would also be expressing something. This time it would be deliberate. Alfred Schutz[34] describes involuntarily activity such as the first simply as 'behaviour' and more conscious activity as 'action'.

[*In the arts we are concerned with helping children to investigate their ideas and feelings, beliefs and attitudes towards the social world of which they are part through their own expressive action, and not just with provoking uncontrolled expressive behaviour as a reaction to a stimulus.*]

Moreover their expressive action in the arts is projected, as Robert Witkin has pointed out,[35] through a particular medium. through paint, through stone, through words, or as in drama, through the medium of their own actions in the depicted world of the drama.

In working through a medium of expression, the individual is guided by a sense of form. But he/she is also guided by a sense of communication. And this helps to take us to the heart of it, I think.

The past emphasis on individuality tended to picture schools rather like plantations with creativity as a kind of fertilizer. Thus children are educated *in* groups but not *as* groups. They are treated as single units. Most of our educational processes emphasize privatized learning. Children sit with their arms around their work taking care not to learn from each other in case they are accused of cheating. The trouble is that, even setting obvious differences aside, children are not like plants. Plants apparently aren't much interested in other plants and stay where they're put even when left alone. Children are and they don't. Like the rest of us, when they are not being kept apart, they live their lives in an intricate entanglement of social contacts, talking and listening, swopping experiences, caught up in a complex web of social values. They do not develop from the inside out, in a cultural vacuum, and the insistence on developing individuals tends to imply that they do. Neither do they just absorb these values from the social atmosphere; they help to create them, and the insistence on self-expression tends to suggest that they do not.

The most important single characteristic of drama in schools, of theatre and of the arts in general is that, like most of what children and the rest of us do, they are social and serve a social function. The use of drama helps to take individual education out of its customary social vacuum and enables children to learn openly from each other in an atmosphere of social interaction. Theatre was discredited in drama teaching because, I think, of a mistaken emphasis on self-expression and individuality which overlooked the social nature of these processes and the possibility of their having more than one function. This is exactly what was implied in the use we made in the Schools Council report of the term the 'negotiation of meaning'. This describes, I think, the central dynamic of drama and its implications reveal how closely drama and theatre activities are related inside and outside the school curriculum.

THE NEGOTIATION OF MEANING

What are we to make of it when Dorothy Heathcote tells a group of children, as she did in her opening session that they only have to 'find a meaning'? Why should it be an interesting, let alone an obsessive exercise for Bill Gaskill to get an audience to describe what happens during an improvisation? If saying what happens simply means pointing out what was there, why should it be so contentious and provide so many different accounts? And why should two observers of Dorothy Heathcote's session with the actors have given the impression that they were at two entirely different sessions?

Part of the reason for these discrepancies both in perceptions and interpretations is that, as George Kelly says: 'the correspondence between what people really think exists and what really does exist is a constantly changing one.'[36] When the deepest divisions and closest affinities between groups and individuals hinge on questions of ideology, attitudes, persuasion and vision, and when the most urgent movements in the social world are triggered and carried on shifts of consciousness, in *ways of seeing*, then I think we have to admit that there may be something in this.

This is not to suggest that there is no objective reality or to fret over whether this really is a radiator I see before me; nor is it to suggest that some ways of looking at things have not proved more useful or productive than others. It is to say that the way we see events, the meaning we make of them, is wholly coloured by the ideas and values *we bring* to them. There may be an objective reality for us to know, but we would be pushed to say just when we had discovered it.

We see the public world from a centre within ourselves, from within a private world of our own consciousness. The recognition that there is a difference between these two worlds is one of the first steps on the child's road to personal autonomy. If we see events differently, it is partly because we see them from different perspectives, from different centres of vision. Our natural acceptance of these divergences is acknowledged in the daily homilies about 'getting into someone else's shoes', 'taking a different view of things' and trying to see things 'as others see them'.

But if differences in perception were really only due to differences in perspective, as soon as we had tried out or discovered everybody's view of a problem, disagreements would be quickly cleared up in a round of hearty back-slapping as we saw the sources of our misunderstandings clearly picked out in the bright flare of an 'objective overview'.

The problem with this idea is that getting everyone's view of an issue is normally only the start of the argument. The more we understand how someone else sees things the more deeply we may tend to disagree. For it is not so much that what we see of something determines how we come to look at it, but rather that how we look at something determines what we actually see. To a naturalist a salmon may be an essential agent in a river's ecological balance: to a fisherman it may be a noble but cunning opponent; to a painter a subtle tango of rippling colour and to a fishmonger so much a pound.

It makes no difference to the fish so long as it is left alone. These differences in perception between individuals and groups, the effects of which can be much less trivial, result from our seeing the world, and our own actions in it through a framework of concepts and values which act as filters on perceptions toning them in to our personal picture of what reality is like. Perceptions, in other words, take place within a framework of conceptions.

There are actual physical limits to our field of perception. These are set by our physical organization which forces us to see the world in some ways rather than others. Just as the sea horse and the killer whale live in the same stretch of ocean but perceive

ly different worlds, we see and live in the world
because of the way we are built. But our
e world – that is, what within our available field
actually pick out and consider as significant or
ningful or meaningless – has no such physical
...y. it is determined by the systems of ideas and values
through which we look at it and these vary as between
individuals, cultures and ideological groups. Moreover these
systems are learnt, for the most part, are culturally specific and,
most importantly, are capable of change.

PERSONAL KNOWING

In seeing the world one way or another we are exercising some
degree of personal choice. Bertrand Russell asked, 'Is man what
he seems to the astronomer, a tiny lump of impure carbon and
water impotently crawling on a small and unimportant planet?
Or is he what he seems to Hamlet? Or is he both at once?'[37] The
alternatives are infinite, according to the evidence we select and
our line of approach. But in Michael Polanyi's words: 'Any
attempt to eliminate our human perspective from our picture of
the world would lead to absurdity.'[38] There is an important
difference between aiming to be objective – that is having a
concern for accuracy – and claiming for what we know that it
represents a final, irrefutable, impersonal truth. In claiming to
know something we are investing it with a personal conviction.
As Polanyi puts it: 'Into every act of knowing there enters a tacit
and passionate contribution of the person knowing what is being
known. . . . This is no imperfection but a necessary component of
all knowledge. . . . Objectivism seeks to relieve us from all
responsibility for the holding of our own beliefs.'[39]

We may try to be objective but we cannot be neutral. The use
of drama in schools to engage the expressive actions of children is
one of the ways of enabling them to confirm these personal
responsibilities by investigating what their beliefs, ideas, attitudes
and feelings actually are.

THE CREATIVE MIND

I described drama, earlier, as an act of representation. A great
deal of our actions in the world involve acts of representation. It

is the characteristic activity of thought to represent experiences in consciousness and to interpret them through a system of concepts. Many of these are inherited, most obviously through learning the spoken and written language of our cultural group. In learning a language, children are not simply memorizing a system of names for the experiences they have and the objects they use. They are also learning the complicated system of relationships of which the language principally consists. They are not just acquiring a way of talking about the world but a system of concepts which will encourage them to construe it, to interpret it, in some ways rather than others. In learning to speak, the child is also learning a culture. But a culture consists of more than a verbal language. Language is just one of the ways in which we represent or symbolize our experience and ideas. Many aspects of our experience of the world and of ourselves are too fine or too precise to be caught in the coarse net of words. For these we use other modes of representation and in the symbolism of the arts and the sciences we develop ways of construing reality which, if less handy than language, are at least more responsive to its complexities.

Scientists and artists alike, and they may be the same people, are equally concerned to get a grip on concrete reality. Both are creative; neither are wholly objective. Because of this we have to be careful in saying that the point of the arts in schools is to make children more creative. 'Creativity' is a myth if we are to think of it as a separate faculty which only springs to life in certain types of activity, like 'art'. We do not have creativity, like we have jaundice, in a measured dose. The activity of mind, if it is active, is essentially creative.

[We do not live in a world of static social realities.] If we did, all creative and expressive actions would simply be spasmodic variations around an unchanging theme. The social world is not an 'abandoned monument' but, as George Kelly puts it, 'an event of tremendous proportions, the conclusions of which are not apparent. It exists by happening. It is hard to imagine what the world would be like if it just sat there and did nothing.'[40] [Our personal construction of reality, in both a literal and a metaphorical sense, is an active rather than a passive process.]

We come to see things as we do partly because of the experiences we directly undergo. But events do not simply happen to us. We make them happen and, in a way, we happen to them: we influence what is going on through our own actions and responses. We are implicated in a continuous process of interaction and negotiation with the ideas and actions of others. We approach new experiences through our existing framework of ideas and values. These may be modified in the light of fresh experience: these changes will in turn effect how we come to make sense of subsequent experience. If we construct a reality to lean on, by means of this continuous dialectic, we are constantly reconstructing it:

> To make sense out of concrete events we thread them through with constructs and to make sense of the constructs we must point them at events. Here we have a full cycle of sense-making.[41]

[We interpret the world as we do through a process of *successive approximations*. This is the basic process of the creative mind: testing new relationships, fresh formulations and novel variations of ideas in the successive interpretation and re-interpretation of experience.] It is the same process at the heart of drama/theatre and of all of the arts and of science. But most importantly, in its broad strokes, it is not a special process at all, but the common way in which we try to make sense of everyday events and relationships.

Although we are born into cultural systems of values and ideas, this basic capacity for creative reconstruction of our personal and – by extension – the public world, means that no-one need be forever a 'victim of their own biography'.

There is always a potential for change. Yet this key dynamic of learning is often suspended, ironically, during education. Children, still, are mostly faced with unilateral declarations of the way things are. In these circumstances the idea of 'self-expression' as a sure route to individuality is a simple deceit.

[Often what passes for self-expression is no more than an unwitting demonstration by children of the values they have inherited and 'the emotions they have been taught to feel'.[42]]

DRAMA, THEATRE AND SOCIAL REALITY

In drama and theatre we envisage other realities and temporarily dwell in them, so as to provide descriptions and observations of real life. In doing this we give credence to events that we know are not really taking place at all.

In watching a play we might simply see a group of men and women walking about a small area, speaking at each other from memory and more loudly than they need given the distance between them. Literally, that is what is going on.

Alternatively, we might just believe that the Prince of Denmark is really there live on stage just as some children may believe, after their first pantomine that they have really seen Dick Whittington in the flesh. But we don't.

We look through the real actions to the events which they represent. And what are represented are examples from and interpretations of actual experiences – or fictitious ones derived from them – which are held up *as objects of reflection*.

This is true of both drama and theatre. Yet there are a number of differences between them. One of these is to do with the sense of convention which guides our involvement: with the way we see the relationship between what is really going on, literally, and what is being represented.

In the theatre there is a clear, generally understood, demarcation between the audience and the actors. This is obvious enough. The clarity of this line is not blurred by whether or not as an audience we get physically involved by being brought on the stage or addressed directly – as some attempts at so-called 'audience participation' have led to. The demarcation is not to do with who sits where or the physical arrangements for the event. It is to do with our own sense of distinction between the actor and the role he is playing.

When we talk of an actor playing a role we do not mean it in the same sense that we have roles in real life: as parents, tax-payers, nephews, nieces and so on. For when we talk of these roles we mean the different rights and responsibilities we assume and the different aspects of ourselves we show according to our status in different social situations. But our actions in these various roles do have outcomes in the real world. The actor's role does not. It is a representation of someone's action in the depicted world of the play.

The actor playing Hamlet is not expressing his own grief, and we know very well he isn't. At the end of the evening we don't send the actor's family our condolences.

But neither is he expressing Hamlet's grief. Hamlet expresses his own grief. The actor represents this act of expression. In doing so he may well be expressing something of himself too.

His involvement with the character will doubtless call on a pro-found sense of identity or empathy with Hamlet's emotions. Nevertheless we know it is Hamlet who is broken at the end and not the actor, who has brought him to life.

If we are moved by the actor's grief we are out of touch with Hamlet. If in the theatre we catch the actor's eye and see him look at us as ourselves or, more importantly as himself, we lose sight of the character. The actor may, as in some performances, move among us in role, but our sense of distinction, of conven-tion, guides us in knowing whether we respond to him or to the character. We don't do both.

This only breaks down when the convention is not under-stood. I once heard of an extreme case of this when a travelling theatre group, in the pioneer days of the American West, were touring a version of Othello. The climax of the show came earlier than usual when a member of the audience, tuning in to how things were going for Desdemona and sensing the need for a firm hand, shot Iago in the third act. This is rare. Except in some examples of 'participatory theatre' where the conventions are constantly shifting – and perhaps this just took the idea of participatory theatre to a natural conclusion – there is no actual interaction between the actors *as themselves*, and the audience.

In the drama lesson the dividing line between the real social roles of the group during the drama and the roles they are depicting is not nearly so clear. In both drama and theatre there are two levels of interaction: (i) a real social interaction and (ii) a symbolic interaction – that is an interaction between the roles which are represented.

In theatre, the division between actors and audience means that the distinction between the real and the symbolic levels of inter-action is also clear. The symbolic interaction is centred on the playing area. Although the audience identify with the roles which are represented, the real interaction between the audience and the actors is limited as a rule to the performers adapting their performance to the audience's responses.

In the drama lesson, however, there is both a symbolic and a real interaction between all of the participants simultaneously. This is not to say, incidentally, that in the drama lesson there is no audience: there is. Although the participants are in role the members of a group work during drama with a strong sense of being audience to themselves and their own actions. In Dorothy's first session the children sometimes referred to The Sailor as 'She' (p. 33). In working with her as the Sailor and as pilgrims, they were still responding to her and to each other as a group working with Mrs Heathcote. This does not mean that their involvement in the drama could not be genuine or productive or that it was shallow, simply that they were participating on two levels at the same time: in both the real world and the depicted one.

If in drama, children can explore a range of symbolic roles, equally the teacher can enable them to experiment with their real social roles in the group: for the interaction in drama does not just happen *at* these two levels but *between* them as well: that is, the symbolic roles may often be used to get some business done at the real social level or to change the actual situation. In Dorothy's second session, one of the boys asked if he could be the corpse. It's unlikely that he had something particular to get off his chest about dead bodies. He was probably trying to lessen his exposure in the group. By apparently moving himself to the centre of the drama he was probably trying to put himself at the edge of it. If you're a corpse, what can you do but lie there? Quite a lot, as it turned out but he wasn't to know that at the time.

I raised earlier the question of why it should be, if dramatizing is so natural, that some children find it so difficult to get involved. I think it is just because of these real social pressures which it creates. Any group has a network of real social relationships. These may range from total unfamiliarity and tentativeness with a new grouping, to long-established sets of friends and rivals with completely fixed expectations of each other in an old one. The actions of a group in a drama session, in role or out of it, are not just a response to what the teacher asks them to do. They are also responses to the expectations they have of each other. We do not simply drop our normal social roles just because we are asked to act-out another one. On the contrary: we now have two sets of roles to handle.

In working with a group for the first time, or with one which is uncommitted to drama, the teacher needs to know how the real social network is operating. Otherwise whatever the group does will only ever make partial sense. For some individuals in some groups taking on certain roles may be all but impossible. At other times, particularly with people who are completely new to drama, it may not be taking on any particular role which proves to be difficult – for example a quiet person being asked to play an aggressive one – but the fact of doing it at all.

Bertrand Russell once compared the social habits of ants with those of human beings and observed that, organizationally, there is not a lot to choose between them, except that they seem to be somewhat better organized than we are.[43] On the other hand they do not produce great works of art, they have not become industrialized as yet and they do not go from anthill to anthill preaching that all ants are sisters, or trying to mobilize the workers on behalf of all antkind. They do not seem to be pre-occupied with metaphysical speculations and they do not form ideological groups. We do. Socially speaking ants have reached a point of evolutionary stagnation and we have not. Nevertheless the rigidity of an insect's universe means it is less prone to sudden collapse than ours through having its basic ideas disproved. Challenging the roles and ideas which hold a group together, which in fact identify it *as* a group, amounts to rattling its whole ideological framework. If a teacher or anyone else presumes to make these challenges in a drama session, by altering roles and shaking the basic assumptions which cement the group together, it is important to offer some support in the process.

Few people, children or adults, will take the necessary social risks which a productive involvement in drama requires, without some sense that it will repay the effort or unless they can be sure, through confidence in the teacher, that in real terms they will not regret it. If they have something to gain by stepping into the middle of such a social arena, they also have something to lose. The alternatives, even in schools, where it may be compulsory, are easily available: sitting back, appearing to be involved, treating it as a joke, not taking part at all. We have to know what we are asking. Children are often asked to get into groups in drama. This is not quite so simple as it sounds. If they don't know each other at all, this can be a very difficult choice. If they know each other very well they may feel that they've got no choice at all. The teacher can easily lose control at this point of one of the most important aspects of the session: that is, *how* the individuals will work together. The teacher is responsible for the social lubrication of the group, making relationships as fluid as possible; creating opportunities for fresh contacts and new ideas. The alternative may be stereotyped responses to ideas from fixed groups and a reinforcement of the existing social roles.

If drama has a potential for changing understanding it does not come about all of itself but through the skill and control of the teacher. The members of a group do not forget who they are and how they normally relate to each other simply because they are asked to take on a role. The depicted world of the drama is unlikely to be revealing unless the teacher, who helps to control it, has a clear understanding of the social reality in which it is based.

ROLES AND FUNCTIONS IN DRAMA AND THEATRE

I began by saying that there is a relationship between the various *functions*[44] of drama and theatre. This is not to suggest that they are the same but that they are in some way connected. How?

Drama is a *process* in a more full-blooded sense than say sculpture or painting because it only ever exists as it happens. But to say that something is a process is to imply much more than that it is a simple sequence of events. These may after all be unconnected in themselves, like the flashing of random slide images on a screen. Calling it a process points to some sort of organizing principle which binds these events together giving them cohesion and unity like the organic imagery of a film. It indicates that each aspect or phase of what is happening is in some sense in every other phase and that 'the future event controls a present activity which uses its past as a means and condition for attaining a later phase in the process'.[45]

The form of a structured play is controlled by the playwright, the director and actors according to a sense of tension and rhythm which guide the pace and pressure of the drama as it unfurls in performance. Gavin Bolton has described how this same sense of form and structure may provide the organizing principle for the improvised exploratory drama of the classroom.

But in addition to these formal characteristics of the process of dramatizing as a whole, there is a range of functions running through it which vary for us according to the capacity in which we are involved in it at any moment. For the purposes of describing them now they have to be extracted for comment one at a time. Nevertheless the point of describing drama as a process is to indicate that each of these functions, and the capacities to which they attach, is in a sense in every other one. The differences in practice are purely of emphasis.

If we set aside our distinction between drama and theatre for the moment and think of the process of dramatizing as a whole we can see, I think, that we get involved in it in three capacities.

We may be, so to speak, the prime-mover, generating ideas and building the drama. We may be re-enacting a drama which has already been devised. We may be involved in any of this as a spectator. We may participate in this process as [*initiator, animator,* or *audience.*]

Each of these roles – in the sense of capacity now – involve certain sorts of activity which have typical functions. The ways in which these functions knit together illustrate the inherently social nature of this process and indicate how artificial and limiting, so far as education is concerned, this rigid dichotomizing between drama and theatre has been.

[*Initiators*

We may be responsible for originating the drama, devising it around our own ideas and feelings, making choices over content and the roles through which to investigate and comment on it. Most classroom drama intends to put children in the role of initiator. The general function of these activities is *heuristic*: they are to do with discovery. In this they are *explorative* – of issues, themes, events – and *expressive* – of attitudes, ideas and feelings about the issues at hand.

There need be no concern at all with communicating to an external audience. This work is not a rehearsal but an enquiry. The drama itself may be disposable. It may develop with a sense of tension and rhythm but also be used only for its immediate value. The conventions allow for easy transitions in and out of role. The drama develops as it goes on: the group is acting-out.

Essentially this is what happens when we dramatise in everyday life. In the drama lesson, however, the process of acting-out is more sustained and takes place, potentially at least, with a more deliberate sense of purpose and form, because it is linked to a set of educational objectives.

Animators

A sculptor or a painter fashions an object which then exists independently. It can be directly experienced by someone else without further interventions. In the performing arts there is an intermediary between the original creative act and its audience: the animator.[46]

An animator is someone who brings something to life and this is precisely the role, in performance, of the musician, the singer, the dancer, the actor. The prime role of the actor is to realize a drama for an audience: to make it be.

The general function of the activity of the actor is to communicate but this is both *expressive* and *interpretative.* The actor is not directly expressing himself as we have seen. He is representing an expression. In this he may identify closely with the character or role and express part of himself through it. But the expressive action of the actor is only part of or a means to his representation of the part. In acting-out, however, it is more often the case that the representation of a role is only part of or a means to the individual's own expressive action.

If acting is expressive, it is also interpretative. Putting children in this role, either informally by showing what they have done to the rest of the class or formally in a structured performance, has been condemned in the past on the grounds that it had neither of these functions.

The following sums up the objections:

> Theatre is an art for showing. In order, for example, to let the audience hear and see, the actor's speech must be louder and the movements larger than in real life and to make [this] seem natural, techniques have to be learnt – techniques so difficult that comparatively few amateur actors master them. The theatre thus imposes severe limitations on self-expression.[47]

As a result, the child actor 'becomes an automaton in the hands of the producer, giving little of his real self to the part and learning little about the real life which it is hoped lies behind the script'.[48]

Is any of this necessarily true? Certainly the skills of the professional actor are complex and sophisticated. But if we compare the nature of the activity to acting-out within the group, despite the obvious differences in skill as between amateurs and professionals, the key difference is really one of function. There is nothing in the nature of the activity itself to suggest that it is less creative or makes fewer demands on the resources of the individual. A text, for example, merely suggests a performance. It does not determine it. Grotowski has observed that:

All the great texts represent a sort of deep gulf for us. Take Hamlet. Professors will tell us, each for himself, that they have discovered an objective Hamlet. They suggest to us revolutionary Hamlets, rebel and impotent Hamlets, Hamlet the outsider, etc. But there is no objective Hamlet. The strength of great works really consists in their catalystic effect: they open doors. . . .[49]

The dramatist may create a self-contained world in the play but he can really only indicate how the people who occupy it look, sound, behave and respond. Giving them living, animate form is left to the creative actions of the actor and this involves a sustained effort of interpretation. A written play, or scenario may present a coherent vision of characters and the events which bind them together but it is impossible 'to derive the performance itself by some logical formula'.[50]

Self-expression is limited because it is not the function of these activities at this point in the process. The emphasis is on communication. But any act of communication in drama as elsewhere would be forever unconsummated without the reciprocal and equally creative activity of the audience who are being communicated to.

Audience

The activity of an audience is both *interpretative* and *appreciative*. The meaning of a play cannot be derived by a logical formula because art is not a *system* of communication. It is not a system at all. There is a difference between a *systematic* symbolism and a *schematic* symbolism, and they make different demands on us in trying to interpret and appreciate them. The symbolism of art is schematic, and the effort of understanding it can be very great.

Spoken and written language and mathematics are examples of systematic symbolism. They consist of signs with conventionalized meanings and rules of structure which govern how they can be put together. In a systematic symbolism there are only certain ways in which the component parts can be put together and still make sense. We may not be able to make out what some sentences actually do mean, but we can generally recognize that they do mean something just in the way they are organized and hang together. And if we meet a new word we can always look it up.

But if we want to understand the meaning of a painting we haven't seen before we can't turn to a dictionary of colours and see what blue and green usually signify when they're put together. There is no manual of significance for the notes of a sonata which will tell us what the whole thing is driving at. No taxonomy of theatrical symbolism exists to decode King Lear for us. There is no fixed use for the symbols of art which divide sense from nonsense. A painting, a play, a symphony, a novel, are single, unique, schematic symbols created out of a sense of essential form rather than of conventional usage. They may be built out of systematic symbols. Plays are written in words after all and there is a system of musical notation. But a script is not a drama and a score is not the music. They are simply cues for them. The work itself has a power beyond that of its component parts. Our response to a poem is not the same as to a piece of technical prose. Not only do we respond to the separate lines and phrases of a poem but also to how it is organized as a complete work. We respond not just to what it says but to how it says it: to its unique form.

In watching a drama then, the audience is not faced with something it can systematically interpret by reading off its symbolism. A drama is open to interpretation on two levels. The audience responds both to what is expressed *in* the play and to what is expressed *by* the play. We interpret what is being expressed *in* the play as it unfolds before us, by following piecemeal the actions and statements of the characters and the events between them. It is only when the whole thing is over that we can begin to make our own sense of what is expressed *by* the play.

I say 'our own sense' because what the play means for us may be quite different to what it means for the writer, the actors, the directors or whoever was responsible for it: or for anyone else. There is no objective Hamlet because there is no systematic link between what the artist intends to express in and through the work and what the work itself expresses for us. The communication which is inherent in a work of art involves at least two creative actions: those of the artist and those of the audience. In the case of the performing arts it involves three. Our perception of a play involves meeting the actions of representation on the stage with a reciprocal act of projection of our own by which we see and interpret them as such. These actions lock together in any act of communication in drama.

Art appreciation is still often taught as if art were a system and understanding it were a simple matter of learning to crack a code. Poetry is often presented to students as a kind of bio-graphical puzzle about the poet. Poems are dissected as if their meaning could be found inside them like the cause of death in a post mortem. But the role of the audience is not just to figure out what the work means to whoever created it, like solving a crime. It is to find out what the work expresses to them. The job of the teacher in this respect is to enable children to have a creative engagement with realized art: to see it as resulting from the same process they are involved in in their own expressive work – and not simply to tell them routinely what everyone else has decided a particular work means, holding it up for passive admiration.

Raymond Williams in *The Long Revolution* points out that artists and scientists are not special classes of people exempt from the normal run of every day events. We all take up the roles of artist or scientist in our dealings with the world. But the emergence of a special class of artists, has weakened the status of the efforts of those who are not in the profession. The work of artists is held up like marvellous cultural curios to be admired. This idea of artists churning out objects for the rest of us to appreciate is a characteristic of aesthetic theory and as Williams says, its tendency is to ignore communication as a social fact, and in doing so to ignore the creative action of the audience.

Communication is the crux of art . . . art cannot exist unless a working communciation is reached, and this communication is an activity in which both artists and spectators participate. When art communicates, a human experience is actively offered and actively received. Below this activity threshold there can be no art.[51]

In singling out these main roles in the process of dramatizing and concentrating on their main, typical functions, I am obviously making a simplification. There are infinite subtleties in the way they blend and merge in practice. The child who turns and shows his improvisation to the rest of the class moves from being primarily initiator to being an animator of his own drama. But the two roles will merge if he begins to create fresh turns in the drama as he goes along. Still he is doing something more complicated now than when working without the external audience because there is now the extra effort of trying to communicate. Those who watch are in the role of audience if only for a brief time before moving back into the role of initiators themselves.

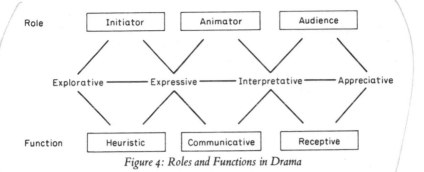

Figure 4: Roles and Functions in Drama

The relationships I can see between these various roles and functions are laid out diagrammatically in Figure 4. This is not supposed to be a picture of drama. If we wanted to try and represent visually how the process operates in practice we would probably want something like a moving spiral. Neither is it intended to mark all of the various nuances of role and function. To do that would produce something like a map of the London underground and not have the same practical usefulness.

A visual display such as this is only useful as a basis for inference. It helps to indicate relationships. The inference I want to make immediately is this: the history of drama in schools has seen different aspects of this process emphasized and approved at different times. The fact that it all carried out being called 'drama' merely indicates that they were only different aspects. Until the movement which was represented by *Child Drama* got under way, the activities indicated by the right hand side of the diagram were most approved and reckoned to hold the greatest educational value. Indeed the alternatives hadn't been much considered except by a few. In the fifties and sixties the swing was to the left of the diagram and only activities to be found there were thought to be helpful. I have tried to argue that the arguments advanced on behalf of these activities – that in themselves, they develop the individual through creative self-expression – overlooked the crucial social nature of learning and the part which the *whole* process of dramatizing, being inherently a social process rooted in communication, can play in this. For a time self-expression seemed to be seen as some sort of terminal condition. Ignoring the other functions and roles which drama makes available to education leaves the whole ideas of drama in education only partially complete.

In a sense the whole of this chapter has been an example of the point I have been trying to make: that the meaning we make of things is not a material quality which we find lying about everywhere, but something we forge for ourselves through the ideas and values we have available. I have been suggesting a particular set of ideas for looking at drama. The diagram is not a picture of drama but a way of thinking about it. George Kelly has pointed out that the physical universe owes no allegiance to any particular theory or way of looking at it. Despite the successive reformulation of the basic physical laws of science the physical world just carries on with the business of happening, regardless. Making sense of it all is our problem. But this is not true of the social world. We construct that in a much more significant way.

We build it through our own actions and these are rooted in the way we see it. The arts play some part in this either by reinforcing or challenging prevailing ideas. One of the consequences of making a special social class out of artists is that what they do has attracted a reverence and sense of other-worldliness which it does not deserve. [Plays, music, paintings are often looked upon as bricks in some sort of public monument to creative achievment or, worse still, as kind of permanent vault of cultural values. Children are introduced to them as if they were holy writ or the products of an alien intelligence. Artists are not on parole from society. They create what they do from their experience as members of it.]

Knowledge is a powerful social weapon and much of education exists to see that children have it. The movement in some schools to make the arts fully respectable has seen the introduction of studies in realized art as examination courses: such as Theatre Arts. I am not advocating a return to purely theatre-based activity but a use of the whole process. The point about the creative role of audience is, among others, that realized art forms can and should be used as both the ignition and fuel for further creative actions rather than as objects of passive admiration. They are the results by others of the very process we are trying to involve children in. This does not mean tagging on a two year course in Theatre Arts at the end of the secondary school, but seeing theatre activities, including plays and performances, as being *available* throughout the work.

The arts are an essential part of the *culture* (in the anthropological sense) in which children develop. Social education means more than putting children into groups of four for ten minutes to find out what they each think about something. It means helping them to understand and reflect on the social values which are pressing in on them, and their part in the dialectics of change.

There is an advertisement on the hoardings for a newspaper which is trying to popularize the phrase, 'Times change values don't'. This may be actionable given the laws on advertising. Changes in value are one of the ways in which we mark the passing of time. Realized art is one of the ways in which we publicly evaluate and promote these changes. Arts education does not simply mean keeping up a stock of appreciative audiences. It is one of the ways in which children and adults concentrate their own creative actions into acts of understanding and evaluation.

But unless professional artists have a receptive, creative audience to communicate to, they will have to find ways of adapting to a growing sense of irrelevance to an increasing majority of people. Encouraging and enabling a greater degree of personal initiative in the arts does not add up to abandoning the cultural heritage. It could be one of the ways in which the functions of all of this art which has been slowly heaped up and admired, will be re-discovered. Art is not important in itself. It is only important if it serves a purpose. And its main purposes are social.

Acknowledgments

I would like to thank the many people who made available their notes and comments on the Riverside Conference. These were invaluable in making plain how the work of the conference had been seen and in highlighting the issues and questions in most urgent need of clarification and development.

I am indebted to the members of the Royal Court Teachers' Advisory Group for leading the discussion groups during the conference and for the written reports which many of them submitted. These included, Tom Swann, Frances Magee, Andrew Bethell, Claire Widgery, Anne Lloyd, and Ron Groom. I owe particular thanks to Cecily O'Neill for access to various tape recordings of the practical sessions.

A number of conference members submitted independent comments including Brian Woolland, Meg Jepson, Albert Labun, Liz Armour, Pam Schweitzer, Ian McKeand, Ken Bartlett, and Dougie Squires.

For their help and advice in other ways I am grateful to E. J. Burton for making available a great deal of valuable historical material on drama in education; to Nancy Martin for her comments on early drafts; to Roy Shaw of the Arts Council and to Peter Gill at Riverside for their detailed responses to the issues of the conference: to John Allen, to Heather Neill, and to Terry Watts. Final thanks go to Jonathan Porritt and the staff of Burlington Dane School for allowing their pupils to take part in the conference.

KEN ROBINSON

Notes

Introduction

1. See *Notes on Demonstration Groups* (p. 187) for further details.
2. From a lecture given in 1974 entitled 'The Arts and the People: Broadening the Base of the Cultural Pyramid'.
3. *Trades Union Congress Working Party on the Arts: a T.U.C. Consultative Document*, T.U.C., Congress House, 1976.
4. Redcliffe-Maud, *Support for the Arts in England and Wales*, Calouste-Gulbenkian Foundation, 1976.

Chapter 1

1. and 3. When I first heard these comments I instantly wrote them down and have since been unable to find a detailed reference for them.
2. Taken from *New Essays* (contributed to the Edinburgh Saturday Post 1827–38), edited by S. M. Tave, Princeton University Press and O.U.P., 1966.
4. E. Goffman, *Frame Analysis*, Harper and Row, 1974; Penguin Books, 1975.
5. The Priest who appears to lead his congregation in worship will still go on with the service even if there is no-one in the church. At least we assume so. The event will observe the same rules, because it takes place within a different 'purity banding'. There may be set times for active participation and others for quiet reflection. But the burden of the future is not lifted. The participants visit the other room only for the chosen actions to take place. In all other respects they stay in the room of their own living. The second room has become a servicing room for this time.

6. 'The Playwright's Song'. The source of this translation is unknown. Another version can be found in John Willett and Ralph Manheim eds, *Bertolt Brecht Poems, Part 2, 1929–38*, Eyre Methuen, 1976 (p. 257).
7. M. Polanyi, *Personal Knowledge*, Routledge and Kegan Paul, 1969.

Chapter 2

1. Nicholas Gorchakov, *Stanislavsky Directs*, New York and London, 1955.
2. William Poel: English actor and producer. Founder in 1894 of the Elizabethan Stage Society. President of the London Shakespeare League and author of several plays and books on the theatre.

Chapter 3

1. For a more detailed analysis of some further aspects of these three lessons see: G. Bolton, *Towards a Theory of Drama in Education*, Longman, 1980.
2. The report of the Project was published as *Learning Through Drama*, MacGregor, Tate and Robinson, Heinemann Educational Books, 1977.
3. It is interesting that at the time I did not interpret this as a distancing technique but as a direct clue that they were interested in finding out what it was like to be fifth years. This misinterpretation led to some inappropriate questioning by me later on.
4. R. W. Witkin, *The Intelligence of Feeling*, Heinemann Educational Books, 1974 (p. 80).
5. One very useful form of safeguard which I did not use on this occasion is to work by analogy, i.e. placing the subject-matter in a different and therefore safer context. The *centre* remains the same but the fiction is different. 'Violence in School' might become symbolized by threats of mutiny from the crew of Columbus' ship or *Tom Brown's Schooldays* or even the Tolpuddle Martyrs.
6. The Russian psychologist, L. S. Vygotsky discusses child symbolic play as self-imposed discipline in J. S. Bruner, A. Jolly and K. Sylva, (eds) *Play*, Penguin, 1976 (pp. 537–555).

Chapter 4

1. If you ever see an uncut version of *Look Back in Anger* or *Entertaining Mr Sloane*, you will be staggered by the sheer length of the piece: an index of how theatre time has shrunk in fifteen or twenty years. Today the maximum length of an act of a modern play seems to be about an hour.

2. As all actors know, the last few words of most plays return the audience to real time. The process is usually assisted by delivering them in a studied (or affectedly casual) rallentando. Applause follows. Anthropologists have pointed out that states of transition in the ceremonies and rituals of many societies are marked by loud noises. However, applause in Western theatres is remarkably time-stressed. If the audience has been bored – i.e. conscious of the passage of real time – they applaud feebly, there being no need for a public tempo to be re-established. On the other hand, to show immense enthusiasm, audiences beat out a tempo in unison. Real time is thus re-instated.

3. Cleopatra does not possess 'infinite variety'. If she did there would be no play. Her behaviour is consistent throughout.

4. A similar parody of laboratory conditions was perpetrated by medieval scientists in a famous experiment designed to find out where mice came from. Suspecting that they were generated spontaneously in heaps of rags, they locked a lot of rags in a room and came back in a month. When they did, they found their thesis confirmed: there were mice everywhere.

Chapter 5

1. Welfare State is a famous 'performance art' group, based in north-west England, and dedicated to creating some kind of ritualistic event (usually out of doors and usually involving primal elements like fire, ice, water, bread etc). One such event involved a horse-drawn caravan trek across England finishing up in a submarine off Portsmouth harbour; another involved flaming torches staked into the sea-bed which were slowly extinguished by the incoming tide.

2. See *On the Everyday Theatre* by Brecht, translated by John Berger and Anna Bostock, Granville Press, 1972.

3. All the quotations by Devine are from his letters and memos to George Christie, the Director of the Calouste Gulbenkian Foundation (UK Branch) in 1962, to whom he was applying for a grant for his proposed 'Development Scheme'.

4. One such play, *Clowning* by Keith Johnstone, was immensely popular with these children but attracted hostility from the sophisticated adult audience which saw it. Those performances in 1965 illustrate clearly how the Studio broke all the rules, advancing a narrative through spontaneous creation that involved everyone, idea piling onto idea in a furnace of invention. The actors only helped steer a process which depended more on creative spontaneity than conventional discipline.

   Much the same idea was employed by Ken Campbell years later during the 1975 Young Writers Festival when he worked with a class from Marlborough Junior School. They created a play using the simple technique of asking 'And what happens next? And what does he say then?' with Ken as question-master and M.C. combined.

5. Devine believed that the theatre should ultimately be offered as a free service, like a library or health facilities.

6. See *Hopes for Great Happenings: Alternatives in Education and Theatre* by Albert Hunt, Eyre Methuen, 1976. Also Roger Lancaster's report 'Moving On' published by the Arts Council of Great Britain, a useful summary of which appears in *S.C.Y.P.T. Journal 3*.

7. See Schedule 3, pp. 56–73, of the Arts Council's report that year.

8. *What Went Wrong? Working People and the Ideals of the Labour Movement* by Jeremy Seabrook, Gollancz, 1978.

9. See Cecily O'Neill's article in *London Drama*, Vol. 5, No. 6.

10. *Evening News*, 21 January, 1977. Leader article headlined: 'Drop This Hot Potato, Mr Chapman.'

11. The private agonies and public wranglings that accompany the successful presentation of a school play are often focussed on the personality of the foolhardy producer! One teacher who was very keen on directing plays in the past felt obliged to give it up when appointed Deputy Head because problems with staff might have threatened her new status.

12. This transport problem cannot be underestimated, linked as it is to the child's experience of the city environment. A

brilliant exposition of this is in Colin Ward's *The Child in the City*, published by the Architectural Press, 1977.

13. This is no isolated phenomenon: see the article on Common Stock's production of *Inside Kid* in *S.C.Y.P.T. Journal*, No. 3 for a revealing account of a theatre company's confrontation with boys in a Borstal.

14. Final speech from *The School Leaver* by 16-year-old Michael McMillan, published by Black Ink Collective, Sabarr Books, 121 Railton Road, London SE24 (1978).

15. One I.L.E.A. official described his decision to 'clean up' the language of a youth theatre performance as 'censorship of language not of content'!

16. The Hollywood model is *Dirty Harry*.

17. The 'family panto', with its oppressive steretypes of women and gays, is no more suitable for children than the tokenist social relevance of 'progressive' children's plays which sink beneath a patronizing welter of fantasy, scenic effects and songs. I overheard a five-year-old ask his father in the interval, 'What will stop them building the prison and factory in the wood?' The play never answered that question preoccupied as it was with transporting the Queen, the Property Developer and Bino the Clown across the Lake of Loneliness to the Hill of Happiness where everyone lived happily ever after. A good example of how fantasy, unrelated to specific social realities, checks rather than liberates the audience's spirit and intelligence.

18. See *The Theatres of George Devine* by Irving Wardle, Cape, 1978, p. 273.

19. 'Art is as real as life is, in every dimension except that of *chance*.' From 'A Light to Learning' by Dorothy Heathcote in *Young Drama*, Vol. 6, No. 2.

20. Final speech from *Not in Norwich*, ed David Lan, Y.P.T.S.

21. Each youth had been beaten up at least once, and in one case six times. Some were members of an illicit Bengali vigilante group.

22. From Writers Workshops Report, published by the Y.P.T.S.

23. There have been several experiments of writers working within the school system. A very good account of some of these is contained in the Education Supplement 'Writers in Residence' published by the Greater London Arts Association, 25/31 Tavistock Place, London WC1.

24. From 'Report on Y.P.T.S. Writers in Schools Project', October 1977, published by the Y.P.T.S.

25. The transcripts are available from the Y.P.T.S.

26. See the report prepared by the 'Children's Theatre Working Party', for the Arts Council's Drama Panel, 1979, p. 18.

27. The Drama Inspectorate of I.L.E.A. issue a sort of popularity table of plays based on the number of children who are studying them for examinations. The figures for 1978/9, using responses from 48% of schools surveyed, showed *An Inspector Calls* by J. B. Priestley at the top with 3,831 students and *Measure for Measure* at the bottom with 6.

28. See, in particular, *Born to Fail* by P. Wedge and H. Prosser, Arrow Books, 1975, and *Unequal Britain* by F. Field, Arrow Books, 1974, and *Learning to Labour* by Paul Willis, Saxon House, 1977.

29. The 'Sus' laws allow police to arrest anyone behaving in a 'suspicious' manner which could, hypothetically, lead to a criminal act. The National Youth Bureau, 17–23 Albion Street, Leicester LE1 6GB, have published a report that seems to show a bias towards arresting young blacks.

30. See also the Greater London Arts Association's Education Supplement on 'Young People and the Arts', G.L.A.A., Spring, 1978.

31. I once witnessed a group of about 25 very young and working-class National Front supporters disrupt a play in the Theatre Upstairs. Beneath the racialist abuse and the chanting of slogans lay a deep-seated class hatred: they despised the apparently middle-class, super-educated audience whose evening they had interrupted and whose accents they derisively imitated. Their daring outburst was like breaching the walls of a culture barracks. It is impossible to imagine the opposite kind of situation, so effectively have the arts been denied to such people. Their tactics of disruption were, in themselves, quite an art.

32. Jeremy Seabrook, *What Went Wrong*, Gollancz, 1978.

33. See also Edward Bond's brilliant essay 'The Murder of Children' in his translation of *Spring Awakening*, Methuen, 1979.

34. The double standard is adequately summed up in Rockefeller's own words, inscribed on a brass plaque outside the Lincoln Center: 'The arts are not for the privileged few, but for the many. Their place is not on the periphery of daily life but at

its center. They should function not merely as another form of entertainment but rather should contribute significantly to our well-being and happiness'.

For a good discussion of the *educational* implications of the cultural poverty/ownership gap see, 'Social Democracy, Education and the Crisis' by Finn, Grant and Johnson, in *On Ideology*, Hutchinson, 1978.

Chapter 6

1. T. H. Vail Motter, *The School Drama*, Heinemann, 1929 (p. 238).
2. Board of Education, *Report on the Teaching of English*, H.M.S.O., 1919 (p. 316).
3. Ibid, p. 316.
4. G. Boas, and H. Hayden, (eds.), *The School Drama*, Methuen, 1938 (p. 32).
5. Ibid., p. v.
6. Ibid, p. v.
7. This estimate was made by John Holgate in an article in *Speech and Drama* (Jan. 1952, Vol. 1, No. 2) published by the Society of Teachers of Speech and Drama. Interestingly enough, after saying that the value of amateur drama was beyond question he adds that many of the plays and productions 'were worthless from an artistic point of view but were important in the social life of the community'. Worthless to whom?
8. These were suggested as being the two principal aims of School Drama at a forum on 'Drama in the School' organized by the Association of Teachers of Speech and Drama (as it was called in the 1930s) at University College London in January 1938. The meeting is reported in the Bulletin of the Association for February 1938 (No. 6). The Bulletin also recorded a meeting of the Association on the subject of 'The Health of The Teacher's Voice' chaired by Dr E. J. Boome.
9. Both lectures were planned by the Association and reported in the Bulletin for February 1937 (No. 3).
10. Board of Education, *Report of the Consultative Committee on Primary Education*, H.M.S.O., 1931, Recommendation 30.
11. Ibid.

184	EXPLORING THEATRE AND EDUCATION

12. This comment was made during the debate on 'Drama in the School' in 1938. See Note 8 above.
13. P. Slade *Child Drama*, University of London Press, 1954.
14. Ibid., p. 25. Peter Slade makes an unusual use of capital letters. Events or ideas he particularly wants to emphasize are given capitals and so always are the words Child and Drama.
15. P. Slade, *An Introduction to Child Drama*, University of London Press, 1958 (p. 2). Following the huge success of *Child Drama*, which is a bulky and detailed book, Peter Slade was prevailed upon to produce a shorter version which would be more accessible to parents and non-specialists. *An Introduction to Child Drama* was the result.
16. He identifies a number of stages in personal development. Sometime during the early childhood is 'the Dawn of Seriousness' for example. But sometime during adolescence the young person suddenly enters what he calls 'The Night'. I'm not sure what event triggers this off. But its effects the following day are that the adolescent takes on the seriousness of the adult.
17. Joint Council for Education Through Art, 'Proceedings of the Conference on Humanity, Technology and Education', held at the Royal Festival Hall, 22–27 April 1957.
18. Ibid, p. 5.
19. Ibid, p. 6.
20. J. Allen, Introduction to G. B. Siks, 'Theatre for Youth: An International Report', *Educational Theatre Journal*, December 1955. Quoted in G. B. Siks, *Creative Dramatics: an Art for Children*, Harper and Bros, New York, 1958 (p. 111).
21. Department of Education and Science, *Education Survey 2: Drama*, H.M.S.O., 1968.
22. Ibid., p. 3.
23. Ibid., p. 46.
24. Ibid., p. 110.
25. J. D. Clegg, 'The Dilemma of Drama in Education' in *Theatre Quarterly*, Vol. III, No. 9, Jan.–March 1973 (p. 33).
26. MacGregor, Tate, and Robinson, *Learning Through Drama*, Heinemann Educational Books, 1977.
27. R. N. Pemberton-Billing, and J. D. Clegg, *Teaching Drama: an Approach to Educational Drama in the Secondary School*, University of London Press, 1965 (p. 33).
28. P. Slade, *Child Drama*, p. 64.
29. Pemberton-Billing and Clegg, op. cit., p. 28. An even more

startling statement along these lines appears in *Child Drama* (p. 73) where Peter Slade says: '[Drama] offers continuous opportunities for playing-out evil in a legal framework and for trying out who you are and what you are going to be . . . it is important that there should be training in the emotions as in the other subjects.' Are the emotions subjects?

30. Government for Northern Ireland Ministry of Education, *Provision for Primary Schools*, Belfast H.M.S.O., 1956 (p. 34). Quoted by Brian Wilks in 'The Joyful Game' an article for *Drama in Education: The Annual Survey*, J. Hodgson, and M. Banham, (eds), Pitman, 1972 (p. 24).

31. A. Tormey, *The Concept of Expression: A Study in Philosophical Psychology and Aesthetics*, Princeton University Press, 1971.

32. Ibid., p. 11.

33. Ibid., p. 22.

34. A. Schutz, *The Phenomenology of the Social World*, translated by George Walsh and Frederick Lehnert, Heinemann Educational Books, 1972.

35. R. Witkin, *The Intelligence of Feeling*, Heinemann Educational Books, 1974.

36. G. A. Kelly, *A Theory of Personality*, Norton and Co, 1963 (p. 6).

37. B. Russell, *History of Western Philosophy*, Allen and Unwin, 1961 (p. 13).

38. M. Polanyi, *Personal Knowledge*, Routledge and Kegan Paul, 1969 (p. 3).

39. Ibid., pp. 312 and 323.

40. G. A. Kelly, op. cit., p. 7.

41. Ibid., p. 122. Kelly also argues that experience does not mean simply enduring. It is made up 'of the successive construing of events. It is not constituted merely by the succession of events themselves. A person can be witness to a tremendous parade of episodes and yet, if he fails to make something out of them, or if he waits until they have all occurred before he attempts to reconstrue them, he gains little in the way of experience from having been around when they happened' (p. 73).

42. M. Polanyi, op. cit., p. 173.

43. B. Russell, *Authority and The Individual*, Allen and Unwin, 1949.

44. Attempts have been made in the past to identify the distinctive aims of drama. This is a pointless exercise. It is another example of the attempts to personify drama. People

have aims, drama doesn't. Drama refers to a certain type of encounter and the activities which produce it. It is no more helpful to talk about the aims of drama than it would be to talk about the aims of theatre or the aims of music. Teachers have aims, playwrights and directors may have aims as individuals. But to try and generalize about what all these aims have in common is futile. Generalizations about the functions of the activities in which they engage is possible however. The difference, I think, is that aims are personal statements which are relatively value-laden and point to desired outcomes of actions. Aims point in two directions: first to the outcomes, and second, backwards to the values of the person whose aims they are. Thus 'to develop sensitivity' tells us as much about the values of the teacher as about the children whose sensitivity he/she aims to develop. To talk of the functions of drama, however, is to make statements about the activities involved and their typical mode of operation. A statement of function is relatively value-free and describes what is happening rather than why it is happening. Functions and aims may coincide but not necessarily. The function of a surgeon's activities in performing an appendicectomy is to remove an appendix. The surgeon's aim in doing it may be to relieve suffering, advance his career, make money or whatever. The patient will have a different aim in having it done. The appendix, having no mind of its own and no values, will not have any aims either, although presumably it once had a function.

45. D. L. Miller, *George Herbert Mead: Self, Language and the World*, University of Texas Press, 1973 (p. 29).
46. In the current jargon of community arts, much use is made of the French word 'animateur' to describe the role of the community artist. I mean no overlap between the two. I'm using 'animator' in its literal sense. I dislike the word 'animateur'. It's implications of injecting life into barren communities strike me as paternalistic.
47. Pemberton-Billing and Clegg, op. cit., p. 18.
48. Ibid., p. 18.
49. J. Grotowski, *Towards A Poor Theatre*, Methuen, 1968 (p. 57).
50. Georg Simmel, 'On The Theory of Theatrical Performances' in *The Sociology of Literature and Drama*, T. Burns, and E. Burns, (eds), Penguin Education, 1973 (p. 305).
51. R. Williams, *The Long Revolution*, Penguin Books, 1971 (p. 42).

Notes on Demonstration Groups

Children's Groups

Both of the children's groups came from Burlington Dane School in Hammersmith and were working with Dorothy Heathcote and Gavin Bolton for the first time.

GROUP ONE WITH GAVIN BOLTON

This first year group had been having one double period of drama each week at school. The teacher described them as being very excited by the idea of working at the conference. They were a single class. The teacher had invited them to participate on a voluntary basis but everybody said they wanted to go.

GROUP TWO WITH DOROTHY HEATHCOTE

This was a very mixed fourth year group. The boys were the last of the old grammar school intake at the school and had had very little experience of drama. The girls had had regular drama lessons up to the end of the third year but none in the fourth. The teacher described them as being a very sceptical and tough group, especially the boys who would not be easily impressed. He estimated that about half of them had come 'for a lark'. They participated voluntarily after signing a notice which had been put up in the school. Consequently they were drawn from all over the school and in many cases didn't know each other at all beforehand.

Actors' Group

The Actors' Group was selected personally by William Gaskill. This was the first time they had worked together as a group. They were: Brian Jennings, Bruce Alexander, Cecily Hobbs, Mary Waterhouse, Philip Joseph, Jessie Gordon and David Pugh.

Select Bibliography

Allen, J. *Drama in Schools: Its Theory and Practice*, Heinemann Educational Books, 1979

Artaud, A. *The Theatre and Its Double*, Calder and Boyars, 1970

Boass, G. and Hayden, H. *The School Drama*, Methuen, 1938

Bolton, G. *Towards a Theory of Drama in Education*, Longman, 1980; 'Creative Drama as an Art Form', in *London Drama*, ILEA, Spring, 1977

Britton, J. *Language and Learning*, Penguin, 1971

Brook, P. *The Empty Space*, Penguin, 1972

Bruner, J. (ed) *Play*, Penguin, 1976

Burns, T. and Burns, E. (eds) *The Sociology of Literature and Drama*, Penguin, 1973

Cauldwell Cook, H. *The Playway*, Heinemann Educational Books, 1914

Chekhov, M. *To The Actor*, Harper, New York, 1952

Clegg, D. 'The Dilemma of Drama in Education' in *Theatre Quarterly*, Vol. III, No. 9, Jan.–March 1973

Contat, M. and Rybalka, M. *Sartre on Theatre*, Quartet Books, 1976

Courtney, R. *Play, Drama and Thought*, Cassell, 1974

Department of Education and Science. *Education Survey 2: Drama*, H.M.S.O., 1968; *Education Survey 22: Actors in Schools*, H.M.S.O., 1977

Dewey, J. *Art as Experience*, Putnam, New York, 1958

Dodd, N. A. and Hickson, W. *Drama and Theatre in Education*, Heinemann Educational Books, 1971

Elsom, J. *Post-War British Theatre*, Routledge, Kegan Paul, 1976

Esslin, M. *Brecht: A Choice of Evils*, Heinemann Educational Books, 1970; *The Theatre of the Absurd*, Penguin, 1968

Field, F. *Unequal Britain*, Arrow Books, 1974

Fines, J. and Ferrier, R. *The Drama of History*, New University Education, 1974

Gascoigne, B. *Twentieth-Century Drama*, Hutchinson, 1962
Goffman, E. *Interaction Ritual*, Allen Lane, 1972; *The Presentation of Self in Everyday Life*, Pelican, 1972; *Frame Analysis*, Penguin, 1975
Gorchakov, N. *Stanislavsky Directs*, New York and London, 1955
Gray, R. *Brecht: The Dramatist*, Cambridge University Press, 1976
Grotowski, J. *Towards a Poor Theatre*, Eyre Methuen, 1975
Hodgson, J. and Banham, M. *Drama in Education: The Annual Survey* (1–3), Pitman, 1972/3/4/5
Hodgson, J. and Richards, R. *Improvisation*, Eyre Methuen, 1974
Hunt, A. *Hopes For Great Happenings*, Methuen, 1976
Jackson, T. (ed) *Learning through Theatre: Essays and Casebooks on Theatre in Education*, Manchester University Press, 1980
Kelly, G. A. *A Theory of Personality*, Norton, New York, 1963
Koestler, A. *The Act of Creation*, Hutchinson, 1964
Laing, R. D. *The Divided Self*, Pelican, 1975
Langer, S. K. *Philosophy in a New Key*, Harvard University Press, 1957; *Feeling and Form*, Routledge, Kegan Paul, 1953
MacGregor, Tate and Robinson. *Learning Through Drama*, Heinemann Educational Books, 1977
Miller, D. L. *George Herbert Mead: Self, Language and the World*, University of Texas, 1973
Miller, S. *The Psychology of Play*, Pelican, 1968
Pemberton-Billing and Clegg, D. *Teaching Drama*, University of London, 1965
Piaget, J. *The Psychology of the Child*, Routledge, Kegan Paul, 1966
Polanyi, M. *Personal Knowledge*, Routledge, Kegan Paul, 1969
Postman, N. and Weingartner, W. *Teaching as a Subversive Activity*, Penguin, 1969
Read, H. *Education Through Art*, Faber, 1943
Reid, L. A. *Meaning in The Arts*, Allen and Unwin, 1969
Ross, M. *The Creative Arts*, Heinemann Educational Books, 1978
Ross, M. *Arts and the Adolescent*, Schools Council Working Paper 54, Evans/Methuen, 1975
Russell, B. *Authority and the Individual*, Allen and Unwin, 1949; *History of Western Philosophy*, Allen and Unwin, 1946
Schutz, A. *Phenomenology of the Social World*, Heinemann Educational Books, 1972
Seabrook, J. *What Went Wrong? Working People and the Ideals of the Labour Movement*, Gollancz, 1978

Slade, P. *Child Drama*, University of London Press, 1954
Stanislavsky, C. *An Actor Prepares*, Bles, 1936
Taylor, J. R. *Anger and After: A Guide to the New British Drama*, Penguin, 1962
Tormey, A. *The Concept of Expression: A Study in Philosophical Psychology and Aesthetics*, Princeton University Press, 1971
Vail Motter, T. H. *The School Drama*, Heinemann, 1929
Vernon, P. E. (ed) *Creativity*, Penguin Education, 1970
Vygotsky, L. S. *Thought and Language*, MIT Press, 1962
Wagner, B. J. *Dorothy Heathcote: Drama as an Educational Medium*, Hutchinson, 1979
Wardle, I. *The Theatre of George Devine*, Cape, 1978
Way, B. *Development Through Drama*, Longman, 1967
Wedge, P. and Prosser, H. *Born to Fail*, Arrow Books, 1975
Willett, J. *Brecht on Theatre*, Methuen, 1964
Williams R. *Drama from Ibsen to Brecht*, Chatto, 1968; *The Long Revolution*, Penguin, 1961
Willis, P. *Learning to Labour*, Saxon House, 1977
Winnicott, D. W. *Playing and Reality*, Pelican, 1971
Witkin, R. *The Intelligence of Feeling*, Heinemann Educational Books, 1974

Line up seat on floor for
possible one later

Two people left with
food, de Henry must
sharger.

Depending
on someone